IDEO
Masters of Innovation

 teNeues

Contents

Published in the U.S. and Canada by
teNeues Publishing Company
16 West 22nd Street, New York, NY 10010
Telephone 212 627 9090
Fax 212 627 9511
www.teneues.com

Published in Germany by
teNeues Verlag GmbH + Co KG
Am Selder 37, 47906 Kempen, Germany
Telephone +49 (0) 21 52/916-0
Fax +49 (0) 21 52/916-111
www.teneues.de

Published by arrangement with
Laurence King Publishing
an imprint of Calmann & King Ltd
71 Great Russell Street
London WC1B 3BP

ISBN 3-8238-5485-2

Printed in Hong Kong

Foreword

Picture the scene. It is spring 1982 and I am sitting drinking beer late on a Friday afternoon in a converted garage in Palo Alto, northern California, with two British industrial designers, Bill Moggridge and Mike Nuttall, who are themselves recently arrived in Silicon Valley. Their design firm, ID TWO, an offshoot of Moggridge Associates in London, has had a busy week. One of many. High-tech entrepreneurs in the area urgently need designers to turn their ideas into marketable products and ID TWO is on a roll.

Moggridge is working on the design of the world's first portable computer, the GriD Compass, and is struggling with the configuration of the folding screen – a design that will later become the international standard. Less than a mile away, a close collaborator of the firm, engineer David Kelley, is developing the world's first computer mouse for Apple.

We crack open another beer. I am in Palo Alto on an assignment from Design magazine. The brief is vague. Talk to designers at the cutting edge of the computer industry. We know something is stirring in Silicon Valley, but what exactly? Can Moggridge, Nuttall and their peers – with their offbeat academic style and playful enthusiasm for electronics – really be at the forefront of a revolution in how we will all live and work? Can a group of laidback designers and engineers in jeans really respond to the corporate needs of the greatest aggregation of venture capital in the world?

As we chat in the fading light, Moggridge and Nuttall aren't convinced they're on the verge of great things, but they're certainly curious about it. They've followed their instincts across the Atlantic and a warm evening in northern California with a full order book is a better place to be for an industrial designer than in recession-ravaged Britain. I drink to that.

We part company and I head off to San Francisco to interview Bruce Burdick, the well-regarded designer of a new system for Herman Miller. 'Keep in touch,' Moggridge calls out, as I stagger off into the night, impressed and intrigued by what I've seen and heard…

Well, I did keep in touch and this book is a result. Bill Moggridge, Mike Nuttall (who set up his own practice) and their collaborator David Kelley worked more and more closely together during the 1980s as Silicon Valley boomed. In 1991 they joined forces to create IDEO.

Another scene. Early 1991, Bill Moggridge in his London office, with a long list of names for the new design firm, trying them out on all his friends and contacts. He's raided the Thesaurus and he wants me to tell him what I think. 'How about Moggridge Nuttall Kelley?,' I suggest, ignoring his list. 'No way,' says Moggridge. 'We want to get away from design personalities. Do something completely different. Develop a totally new innovation process. Here, what about Ideo? It's Greek for idea, you know.'

The rest, as they say, is history. In Silicon Valley, where IDEO has most vividly expressed its innovation talents, that history has unfolded rapidly. This book presents a picture of one of the world's most creative and technically sophisticated design firms on its tenth anniversary. It sets out to capture a decade of IDEO's ideas, experiments and achievements, but as you see, its roots go back much further than that.

I am indebted to Ingelise Nielsen and Tim Brown in London for their special help and support in developing this publication; also to Whitney Mortimer, Scott Underwood and Lynn Winter in Palo Alto, and Simon Cowell at publishers Laurence King, for their expertise and advice. But, perhaps most of all, I am grateful for that first beer in a garage in Palo Alto…

Jeremy Myerson
London, Autumn 2000

We went to the largest and probably the most innovative product design firm in the world and gave them the toughest problem we could think of

Ted Koppel, ABC News

On the evening of 9 February 1999, something remarkable happened on American network television. Instead of the usual half-hour news programme devoted to the latest narcotics bust, political fundraising scam or school shooting, one of the largest US networks, ABC News, devoted its entire 30-minute <u>Nightline</u> news documentary to the issue of how to design new products. The programme, called 'The Deep Dive', focused exclusively on the creative development process of a group of designers in Silicon Valley, described by ABC News anchorman Ted Koppel as 'probably the most innovative product design firm in the world'. That firm was IDEO.

The thrust of the documentary was simple. ABC News threw down the gauntlet to IDEO chief executive officer David Kelley to design and construct a more innovative shopping trolley in just five working days. It was a tough brief. Millions watched coast to coast to see what IDEO's multi-disciplinary team of designers, engineers, researchers and anthropologists would come up with at their headquarters in Palo Alto, northern California. Could they work wonders in just one week to find a way round a familiar but daunting design problem? Or would their limitations in designing for the real world be ruthlessly exposed by the cameras?

It was a gamble, but IDEO rose to the challenge. The team not only built a better shopping trolley in just five days, but also revealed a unique process of innovation that went against the grain of all that corporate America has traditionally stood for. The impact of the ABC <u>Nightline</u> documentary not only confirmed the unrivalled international status of IDEO as multinational industry's busiest, boldest and best-known innovators; it also showed its counter-cultural tendencies. Since engineer David Kelley founded the organization in 1991, IDEO has been on a mission not just to serve business, but to reform it.

Kelley himself signalled as much right at the start of the ABC News programme when he explained that the key characteristics of American industry were to defer to the boss, to climb the corporate ladder and to discourage chaos. At IDEO, he had set this kind of thinking on its head, because all of these things held back innovation. 'Is the boss always going to have the best ideas? Not likely,' snorted Kelley, adding that you've got to hire people who don't always listen to you and that status should be about who comes up with the best ideas, not where they are in the corporate pecking order. As for chaos, 'we encourage craziness because it sometimes leads to the right ideas'.

IDEO's radical theories were put to the test on the shopping trolley project. Did it matter that the firm had not worked in this retail area before? Apparently not. 'We're not actually experts in any given area,' explained Kelley, 'but we're experts in the process of how you design stuff. A toothbrush or a tractor or a space shuttle or a chair, it's all the same to us.'

This is how the shopping trolley project panned out in front of the cameras. Day one saw Kelley and project leader Peter Skillman introduce the task to a large and noisy IDEO team and swiftly orchestrate a focus on key design issues such as safety and security: apparently 22,000 child injuries a year are caused by shopping trolleys, they can travel at 35mph in a gusting wind in a parking lot and they are frequently stolen to serve as mobile storage or barbecues.

Is the boss always going to have the best ideas? Not likely

The designers were then urged to get out of the studio and talk to people who use, make and repair shopping trolleys – another point of difference from mainstream business practice, which tends to value people who are always visible at their desks. 'It's much more useful to get out into the world,' said Peter Skillman, describing the actions of his team as 'people going out to the four corners of the world and coming back with the gold keys to innovation'. At the end of the day, the team reassembled to share these keys: existing shopping trolleys were hard to steer, expensive to maintain, easy to steal, difficult to load and unload, and unhygienic and dangerous for young children.

Day two was devoted to feeding the insights gleaned from shoppers, store owners and trolley manufacturers into a brainstorming session known as the 'deep dive' – a total immersion in the problem. Such brainstorming sessions at IDEO, it was explained to ABC News viewers, run with just five rules: one conversation at a time; stay focused; encourage wild ideas; defer judgement; and build on the ideas of others. Ideas poured out from this session and were pasted on the walls in a series of Post-it notes. The team then voted on their favourite ideas. 'Enlightened trial and error succeeds over the planning of the lone genius' was how one participant summed it up.

Eventually, under the direction of Kelley and Skillman, the 'deep dive' resulted in the formation of four separate groups to focus on four different problems: shopping; safety; checkout; and finding what you are looking for in the store. Calling on IDEO's extensive in-house modelmaking and rapid prototyping facilities, each group built a working prototype to express their ideas and address a certain problem. These concepts were reviewed and the best ideas went forward into a second round of prototypes. Another review, another round of prototypes and so it went on.

We encourage craziness because it sometimes leads to the right ideas

IDEO works on product development for some of the world's major high-tech corporations. Shown here, the Dell Optiplex, reflecting a new design language for Dell computers and accessories.

Building crude, approximate but usable models that can be evaluated in use was shown to be central to the IDEO design process, encapsulated in the motto 'fail often in order to succeed sooner'. Another key factor was the working studio environment itself: quirky, personalized, creative, with suspended aircraft wings, bicycles on ropes and not a standard corporate workstation in sight. 'Being playful is hugely important to being inventive,' explained David Kelley. 'Fresh ideas come faster in a fun place. People here are encouraged to build their own work areas.'

By day three the IDEO team was ready to assemble the final design incorporating all the best elements to emerge from its free-wheeling, multi-disciplinary approach. Over the next two days, a completely new-style shopping trolley took shape. And on day five, as promised, after a night of frantic welding and finishing, it was triumphantly revealed to the Nightline TV audience.

The new trolley was designed to cost the same to manufacture as a traditional one, but it was different in every other way. In concept, it was a steel frame without a basket, incorporating a push handle and side hooks for free-hanging shopping baskets. The thinking behind this was that the trolley would be worthless without a basket and therefore less desirable to steal. A set of small, modular, plastic hand baskets that stack in the metal frame was provided to enable shoppers to protect sensitive items by placing them in different baskets and to leave their 'shopping centre', taking just a small basket to far corners of the store to shop for certain goods. The smaller baskets also eliminated the need to reach into one deep one when putting items into the trolley, producing them at the checkout or loading them into the car.

The new trolley incorporated a moulded plastic child seat, wide enough to carry two children and with a central drawbar to secure them when pulled down. A play surface for children and a writing surface for adults was set into the drawbar. Other notable features included steerable back wheels, so enabling the trolley to be steered sideways out of a tight spot in the store, and a rubber sleeve around the frame to eliminate damage to cars in the parking lot. Looking to the future of shopping, IDEO designed a high-tech scanner in a side holster for the time when shoppers can scan in their own purchases and avoid the checkout queue. The scanner could also provide an audio link to store personnel for advice on where to find items.

Enlightened trial and error succeeds over the planning of the lone genius

IDEO worked with Korean manufacturer Samsung to develop Samsung TotalMedia, a concept project for a home/office multimedia device which combines computing with audio/stereo, telephone, TV and video game playing.

IBM Aptiva Mini Tower: IDEO created the industrial design for this computer processing unit.

Not only did the new trolley offer a host of innovative features and improvements, it looked great too. Store personnel interviewed by ABC's reporter said the IDEO design needed refinement (which was unsurprising given the short timescale involved) but that they really liked it. They clearly identified with the problems it was trying to solve.

By going behind the scenes at IDEO, the Nightline documentary revealed an innovation blueprint for US industry based on the ideas that chaos can be constructive, the boss doesn't have all the answers and that teamwork, not hierarchy, is all-important. The programme also brush-stroked in a number of other major themes, such as the way IDEO has pioneered the coming together of a range of design, engineering and human science disciplines under the umbrella of innovation; its unique culture and environment, which has enabled it to sell not just the results of its innovation process, but the process itself to large corporations; its track record in designing more than 3,000 products for industry worldwide; its growing focus on designing the experience of using a product or service, not just the object itself; its willingness to develop speculative concepts, often at its own cost, which take risks and advance thinking in key areas; and finally, its determination to act as a prototype for the product design firm of the future, rethinking what design practice is all about in the 21st century. All of these themes are discussed in subsequent chapters of this book, and illustrated with relevant projects from IDEO's extensive portfolio.

Today there are around 350 IDEO staff worldwide – a beguiling mix of industrial designers, engineers, computer scientists, cognitive psychologists, human factors specialists, modelmakers and interaction designers of electronic media. The firm has an annual turnover of $60 million and a client list that reads like a global 'who's who' of industry. Nike, Pepsi, Amtrak, BMW, NEC, Steelcase, Seiko, Samsung, GM/Hughes, Yamaha, Canon and Nissan are just a dozen of the 200 or more major companies with whom IDEO has worked. ABC News went to the largest and most influential product design firm in the world and gave it the toughest problem it could think of. And the wheels didn't come off the trolley.

Being playful is hugely important to being inventive. Fresh ideas come faster in a fun place

Shopping trolley designed in just five days for <u>Nightline</u> TV documentary on ABC network. A large American television audience watched the way in which the firm's multi-disciplinary team of designers, engineers and human science researchers worked collaboratively and swiftly to develop a completely new approach.

The result was a product which incorporated clearly identified user benefits.

In a high-profile project for Pepsi, new concepts were designed for buying and consuming cold beverages. The Twist 'n Go Cup is a 32-ounce plastic container that replaces the familiar wax-and-paper cup used for take-out drinks. The cup's distinctive features include a domed removable top, a 'sip lid' that can be closed to prevent spills, and a moulded bottom designed to fit in car cup holders.

Oral-B toothbrushes, developed following observations of young children (and their parents) brushing their teeth. The design team introduced brightly coloured rubber grips, making the toothbrush easier for young children to hold in the correct position and at the same time making the product more fun and 'alligator-like'.

This AirTouch system, designed for US medical manufacturer Midwest Dental, allows dentists to remove tooth decay in seconds with a precise spray of pressurized air. The product's professional and neat look contrasts with the threatening image of most dental equipment.

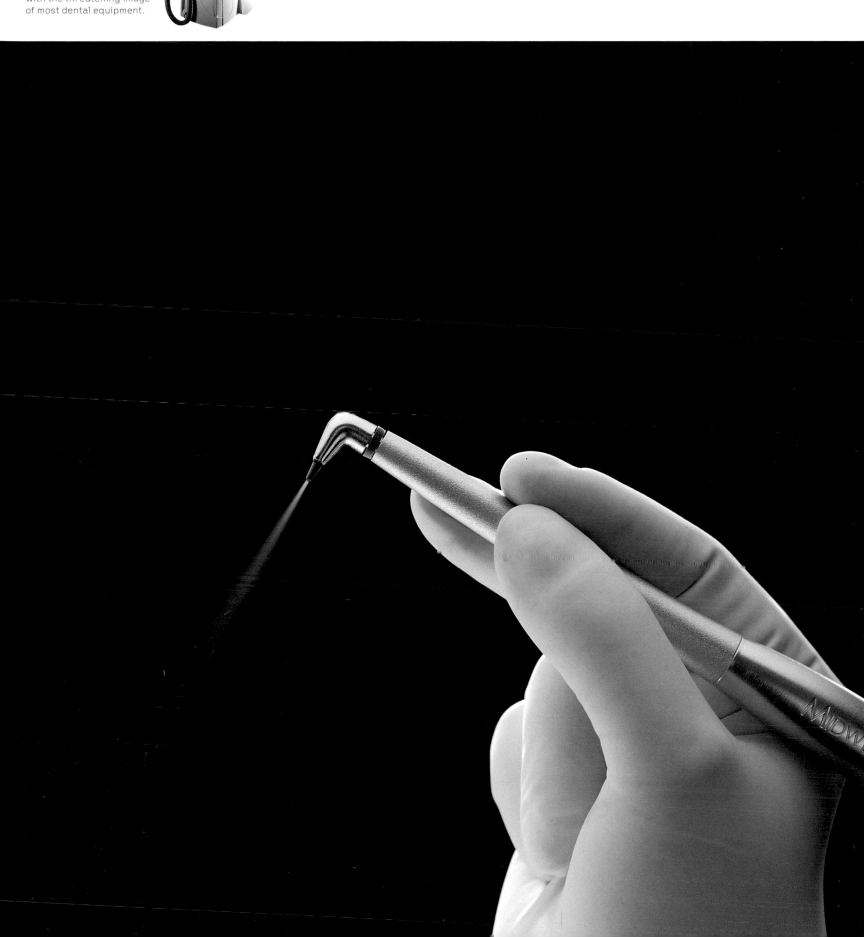

016

SimpleMedia, developed with Samsung Electronics, presents an integrated concept for computer, television, DVD, fax and telephone. Designed as a concept of things to come, SimpleMedia won an award from the ID Magazine Annual Design Review in 1998.

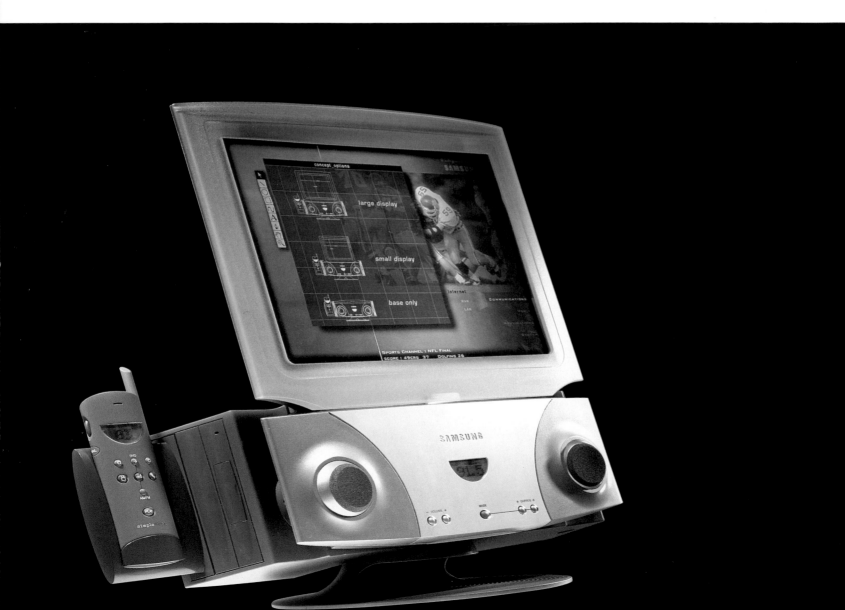

Samsung SyncMaster
400 and 500 TFT monitors,
reflecting an identity for
LCD flat-screen multimedia
monitors. The conical
base has built-in speakers.
The project received
Korea's highest industrial
design award.

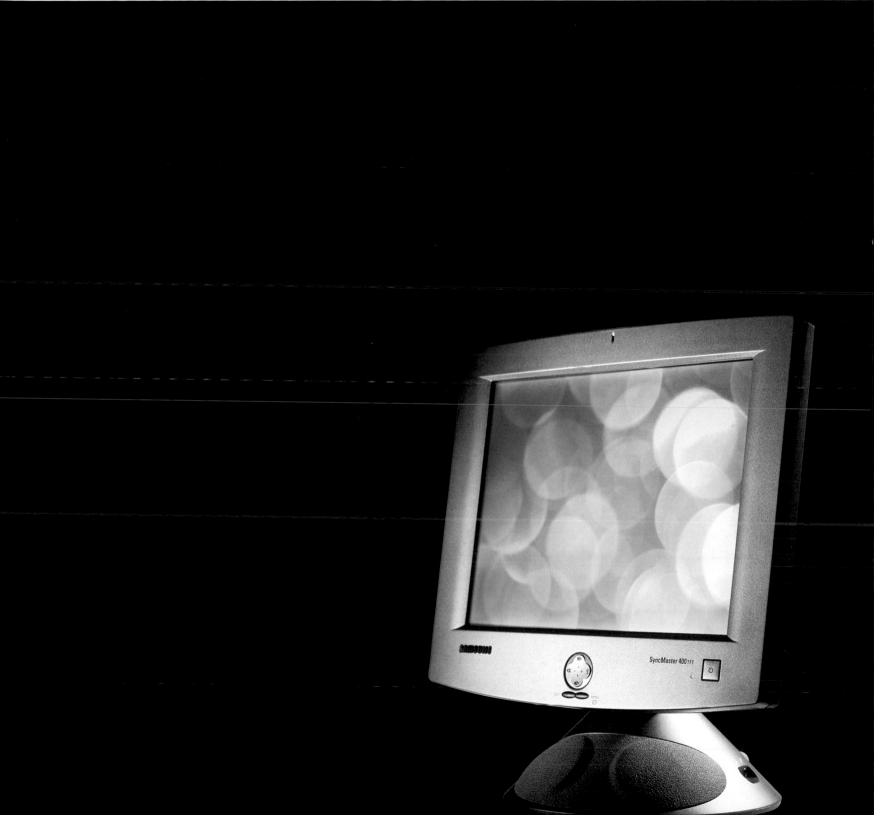

2 Come together

The convergence of factors which created Silicon Valley were unique: the academic institutions, the entrepreneurial spirit, the early successes, the weather...

Larry Lopez, Silicon Valley Bank, California

Mike Nuttall: British industrial designer who brought his Palo Alto-based product design firm Matrix into the IDEO fold in 1991.

Bill Moggridge: leading British designer who followed his instincts that the chip-makers of Silicon Valley would move into high-tech products.

To meet the needs of its clients, IDEO has an international network of 12 design studios on three continents. But five of these are sited down one street in the small and pretty town of Palo Alto in northern California. For all its global pretensions, the firm is most closely identified with this single locality and with the high-tech innovation that has replaced the orchards of the Santa Clara Valley. IDEO has been described by Fortune magazine as Silicon Valley's secret weapon. As Silicon Valley prospered in the 1980s, no longer making chips but new products, so too did the three principals – American engineer David Kelley and two British industrial designers, Bill Moggridge and Mike Nuttall – who came together to form IDEO in 1991.

A further five IDEO studios are today located in other US cities: San Francisco, just an hour's drive to the north of Palo Alto; Boulder; Chicago; Boston and Grand Rapids. Two can be found in Europe – London and Munich – and a Tokyo studio attends to the Far East. In addition, IDEO has affiliate offices in Tel Aviv. But it is Palo Alto that remains IDEO's powerhouse. Located right next door to Stanford University, which has provided many of the high-tech brains for new ventures in the region over the years, IDEO's Palo Alto campus of design studios, electronics labs, model shops and rapid prototyping facilities – 'the street where we live' – has done more to convince the industrialists and venture capitalists of corporate America of the firm's capabilities than anything else.

According to Larry Lopez, senior vice-president of the Silicon Valley Bank, who has been associated with many of the region's high-tech start-ups, including Amazon.com, Cisco Systems and Bay Networks, IDEO is today the top product design firm in Silicon Valley. IDEO's founders positioned themselves in just the right place at just the right time to catch the wave of innovation sweeping through the region. But was it luck or judgement that enabled Kelley and his partners to tap so deep a well of creative and financial capital? In a way, the story of how IDEO came together to unite the disciplines of industrial design and engineering mirrors the spirit of convergence of Silicon Valley itself.

Larry Lopez offers his own assessment from the perspective of running the largest independent bank in the strongest technology innovation region in the world. 'The convergence of factors which created Silicon Valley,' he explains, 'were unique: the great academic institutions; the entrepreneurial spirit that is part of the culture of the region; the weather – people like to live there; and the early successes that meant that capital was recycled – Silicon Graphics spun Netscape, for example.' Lopez describes Silicon Valley's success as an unrepeatable phenomenon – despite the regular trade missions from other economies in the world to study how it was done in the hope of replicating its success elsewhere – and its stellar performers as people with genuine vision and entrepreneurial flair.

Into this hothouse environment came David Kelley, Bill Moggridge and Mike Nuttall with the design and engineering ability to turn new technological ideas into marketable artefacts. By the time IDEO was set up following a merger of their respective product design firms, the trio had already laid down their marker in the Silicon Valley community. David Kelley Design had developed the world's first computer mouse for Apple in 1982, for example, and Moggridge Associates had developed the world's first laptop computer, the GRiD Compass, in the same year.

David Kelley was the main driving force behind the creation of IDEO and his reasons for doing so reveal a lot about his design philosophy. Kelley set out to be an engineer. He studied electrical engineering at Carnegie Mellon University in Pittsburgh, Pennsylvania, and then worked for Boeing where the limitations of engineering rapidly became apparent to him. Despite developing the 'lavatory occupied' signage for the Boeing 747 (an innovation for which a great many passengers are truly grateful), Kelley hated his first job. He was frustrated by departmental silos between different job functions and by an edict from his boss forbidding him to seek advice from the guys in manufacturing because it would make the engineers look stupid.

Kelley realized early on that he really wanted to be a product designer

David Kelley: an engineer by background whose powerful vision of integrated product development was the driving force behind IDEO's formation.

Kelley realized early on that what he really wanted to be was a product designer working in a multi-disciplinary environment where you could talk to anyone you wanted. So he headed west to Palo Alto in 1975 and joined the two-year Masters Program in Product Design at Stanford University. 'I just fell in love with that stuff so much,' he recalls, 'that when I graduated in 1977, I stayed on for another year to do a PhD.' While Kelley was studying, Silicon Valley was starting to happen. Kelley's first commercial venture was the Intergalactic Construction Company, a building demolition firm run by Stanford students. Then, in 1978, he set up his first consultancy, David Kelley Design. Stanford's then Professor of Product Design, Bob McKim, gave Kelley his first client projects. Today Kelley has McKim's berth at Stanford University and combines the demands of a professorship with the rigours of running IDEO.

In the late 1970s, David Kelley Design swiftly found its feet as Silicon Valley was flooded with people seeking engineering help for their high-tech start-ups. Through another Stanford connection, Kelley began to develop telesensory reading systems for blind people. In 1979 he met Apple Computer founder Steve Jobs in Palo Alto – their relationship was to result in the development of the first Apple mouse (later Kelley's company would engineer the sleek black cubes of Jobs' NeXT computer venture). That same year, Kelley was working at a lathe in the workshops at Stanford when in walked Bob McKim with an English designer on a visit to Silicon Valley. The designer's name was Bill Moggridge....

Freeze frame at this point and rewind back to London in the late 1960s. Moggridge had studied industrial design at the Central School of Art and Design and worked for Hoover as a young designer. In 1969 he set up his own firm, Moggridge Associates, and very quickly expanded to work in ten European countries, supported by a retainer from ITT. Moggridge Associates gained a reputation for product design work that was technically precise and visually sophisticated, but in the 1970s, as Britain's industrial base crumbled, Moggridge found himself having to go further and further afield to find projects.

Initially Moggridge thought he might diversify into retail and communication design, as other British designers were doing at the time. But instead he stayed loyal to his discipline and devised a different strategy for survival. He decided to open an American office, having worked for a medical company in Pennsylvania as an award-winning student many years before. In 1978 he took his family for a summer holiday to the East Coast to investigate where the new venture should be located. As Moggridge travelled around in a station wagon, the Boston area seemed the likeliest place. But then a professional contact, John Ellenby, the founder of GRiD Systems, told him about the burgeoning opportunity in Silicon Valley which was just starting to switch from making chips to making products. Moggridge's user-focused design skills would be in greater demand there than in Boston, Ellenby reasoned perceptively.

So Moggridge headed west to northern California in the autumn of 1979: 'I just got the feeling that Silicon Valley would work.' He visited Professor Bob McKim at Stanford University and showed his portfolio. McKim offered Moggridge some part-time teaching work while he looked for clients, and the British designer began to spend ten days every month in Silicon Valley. He rented a home in Palo Alto and named the American branch of Moggridge Associates, ID TWO. However, the early going was slow. Despite many promises, Moggridge won no work at all for three months. 'It was nerve-wracking,' he recalls. 'I had to defer the salaries of my designers. Then at last an engineering company called Calma offered me work and GRiD Systems followed shortly afterwards.'

While Moggridge, widely regarded as among the product design élite in the UK, was scrambling for a precarious professional foothold in Palo Alto in 1979, he walked into the workshops at Stanford University with Bob McKim one day, and there, standing by the lathe, was David Kelley. The two struck up an understanding immediately. David Kelley knew how things worked in Silicon Valley, which was useful to Moggridge. Bill Moggridge, the older of the two, brought sophisticated design standards from Europe, which was useful to Kelley. 'I didn't really know how bad I was as a designer until I met Bill,' says Kelley. 'He told me to go to Europe and visit leading design groups. He did a lot for me personally. And once I saw the work of Bill's studio, ID TWO, I thought I'd be much better off joining him than fighting him. There was a sensitivity to form, better than anything I'd seen.'

I just got the feeling that Silicon Valley would work

The Royal College of Art, London: IDEO looked to its pioneering Computer Related Design course to source the hybrid mix of design and programming skills it required.

So began a period of close collaboration between David Kelley Design and Moggridge. Kelley, the acknowledged market leader in engineering product design, actually spread the projects around a number of industrial design firms, including ID TWO and German designer Hartmut Esslinger's frogdesign, which had also opened a studio in northern California. Things were hotting up nicely in the Valley and there was plenty to go around. By the end of 1982, Moggridge was no longer scratching about for work. In fact, he was wrestling with a client conflict between GRiD Systems and another technology company, Convergent. His solution was to spin off a separate industrial design firm from ID TWO to handle the Convergent project. This breakaway was called Matrix and it was headed by another English designer, Mike Nuttall, who had joined Moggridge Associates in 1977 and followed his boss out to California to work on the GRiD Systems project in 1980.

Under Nuttall's stewardship, Matrix too flourished. 'The main thing about Silicon Valley is that there's a high level of optimism,' says Nuttall. 'I would never have started a design firm in the UK. In the early 1980s there was zero optimism in Manchester.' By the time David Kelley started to work on a landmark computer mouse for Microsoft in 1987, a pattern of regular three-way collaboration had been established between his firm, ID TWO and Matrix. Each practice knew how the others worked. Information flowed routinely between the three.

Gradually, Kelley began to conceive the idea of bringing the three separate entities together to bridge the engineering–design divide: 'I was so far ahead of the game that I had no competitors in engineering design. But when I talked to business people, they told me that I was top of an industry that didn't exist. Clients didn't want to referee a fight between engineers and designers in developing a new product. They wanted an integrated one-stop design consulting firm. So I decided to give up my unique position and merge with Bill Moggridge and Mike Nuttall. I also wanted to join an industry with a higher profile, with award schemes. Industrial design provided all of that.'

The main thing about Silicon Valley is that there's a high level of optimism. I would never have started a design firm in the UK

Stanford University, an academic centre of excellence which developed close links with IDEO. David Kelley is today a professor in the Product Design programme.

To create a new identity for the firm, Kelley travelled to the Connecticut home of the legendary graphic designer Paul Rand to seek a recommendation on who should undertake the work. Rand had designed the IBM striped logo in the 1950s as well as the identity for Steve Jobs' NeXT company. Rand was synonymous with high-tech enterprise, but Kelley didn't presume that the great man himself would be interested in designing an identity for IDEO. However, when Kelley outlined the project and the fee involved, Rand unhesitatingly volunteered himself for the task. The resulting building-block visual communication system, customized by each studio to provide a sense of individuality within the corporate whole, has represented IDEO graphically ever since, even though it has been through periodic updates.

The new super-firm was launched with an understatement typical of its laidback jeans-and-sneakers leaders in spring 1991. From the start it was an international consultancy with 120 staff. Moggridge's London office joined a network which even then included Boston, Chicago and San Francisco studios as well as the Palo Alto headquarters. But while the coming together of IDEO in 1991 marked a landmark, Kelley believes the firm has been through several other landmarks since.

'Our chief characteristic has been that we constantly reconfigure what we do in order to catch the wave of what is new in industry,' he explains. In 1991 IDEO caught the wave of demand from clients to tie up engineering and design as part of a united offer. A few years later it caught the wave again with its pioneering work in the growing but problematic area of computer interface design. The third wave IDEO caught was what academics and economists term 'the experience economy', with its emphasis on designing experiences, not just products or services. On the eve of its tenth anniversary, IDEO is currently 'catching the wave' again as it moves upstream in the development process in order to become more involved in designing the business strategy that comes before designing the product.

Back in 1991, as IDEO concentrated on making sure that the divergent cultures of design and engineering were fully integrated and that designers and engineers shared the same space physically and conceptually, the idea of having business strategists on board as well hadn't yet kicked in. But already the firm was developing a kind of flexibility, a suppleness, that has enabled it since to shift direction into new areas without losing its focus and consistency in total product design.

Within two years of its launch, Fortune magazine included IDEO in an influential survey of '25 cool companies'. It described cool as 'one of the defining characteristics of information technology, a business where insight and creativity can lure lightning bolts from the ether. What's cool? Exciting ideas brought to life. Hanging ten over technology's leading edge. Risk. Breaking the rules and winning. Getting rich without sacrificing humanity.' All of which summed up IDEO, an amalgam of talents calculated to constantly arouse the curiosity of the Silicon Valley's entrepreneurs.

Clients didn't want to referee a fight between engineers and designers in developing a new product

The world's first laptop
computer, the Compass,
designed for GRiD Systems
by Bill Moggridge's ID TWO.
Launched in 1982, its
design configuration with
folding screen set the
international standard
for laptop computing.

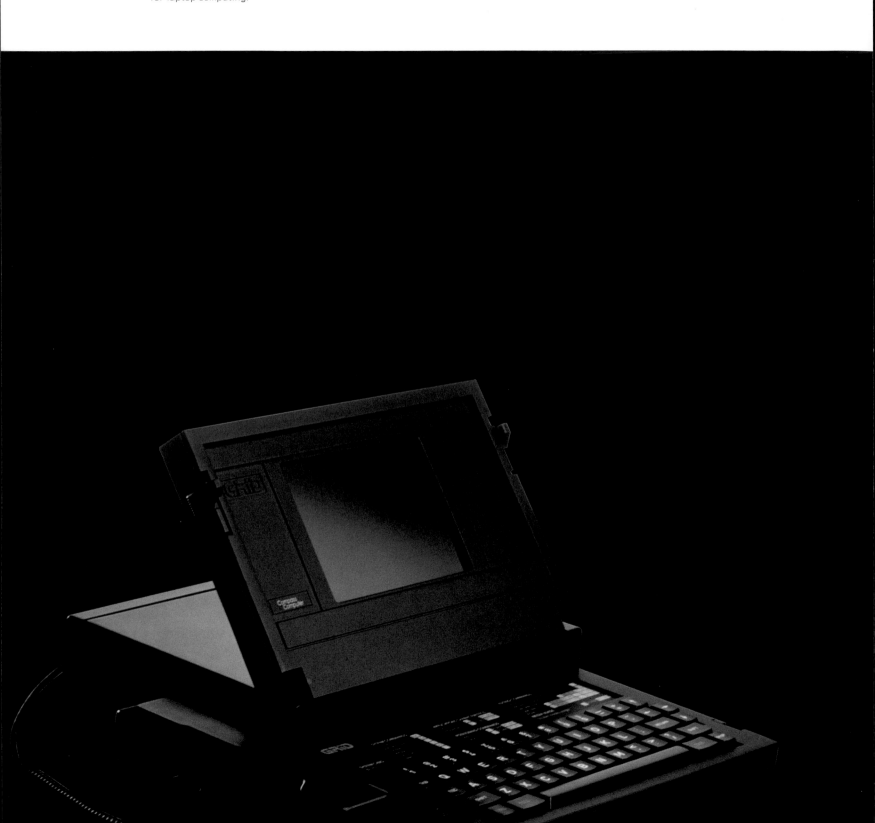

GRiD Systems' patented hinge system, designed and engineered by Bill Moggridge and Steve Hobson at ID TWO. The hinge allows the screen to fold down over the keyboard. The licensing of this patent has been very profitable.

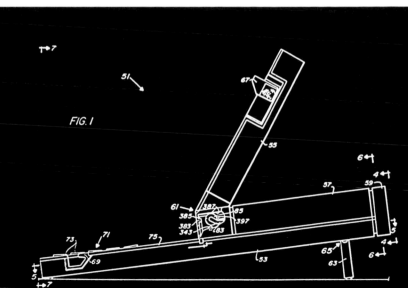

The first Apple Computer
mouse, a ground-breaking
piece of engineering
developed in 1982 by
David Kelley Design.
It was the first computer
mouse in the world to be
produced in quantity.

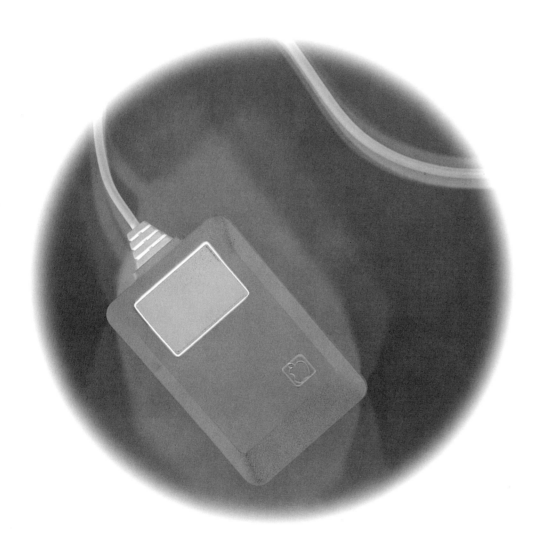

A variety of concepts for the Microsoft Mouse, embodying a working alliance of the three design firms that would later come together to form IDEO. The Microsoft Mouse, destined to be a market leader in terms of performance, ease of use and market share, was designed by Matrix, with human factors research conducted by ID TWO and engineering by David Kelley Design.

3 Focused chaos

Of all the companies I've looked at and written about, IDEO is the only one where I'd love to work

Tom Peters, Tom Peters Group

IDEO's unique culture is rooted in location and communication. View of Golden Gate Bridge near the San Francisco studio.

Right from the start, IDEO's founders recognized that their special way of working, based on building a culture and environment dedicated to fast-tracking the innovation process, could be more than a means to an end. It could be marketable in its own right to large companies that had lost the ability to be flexible, spontaneous and creative, and had become too cumbersome and bureaucratic in developing new products.

According to David Kelley, the larger the company, the greater the barriers to innovation. 'Much of our work,' he explains, 'is in teaching big companies to act small. In the old days, a toaster company would come to us and ask us to design a new toaster. Now companies come to us and say, "How can we make our company more innovative on a routine basis?" That has become the big management question, especially in the States where many companies have appointed a head of innovation.'

Even the global business recession of the early 1990s which greeted IDEO's formation, ironically worked in the firm's interests. The ruthless downsizing of design and engineering departments, which large corporations undertook to survive, destroyed their own capacity to innovate. Once the economy improved and reducing costs was no longer the only show in town, they needed external help from firms like IDEO to add value in terms of new ideas.

That thinking explains why US office furniture giant Steelcase Inc., one of IDEO's clients, took an undisclosed equity share in the firm in 1996. When IDEO launched in 1991, David Kelley owned the firm 100 per cent, having bought out his co-founders. Steelcase's capital investment enabled IDEO to expand and enhance its resources. 'The reason why a large corporation like Steelcase became interested in IDEO was not the profits we could make for them,' explains Kelley. 'It was because we could help them to be more innovative. When you're a $3 billion company, being just 1 per cent more innovative is important.' Steelcase chief executive officer Jim Hackett confirms the attraction of what has been termed 'the science of creative fun' at IDEO: 'You have to ask yourself why people like Jim Hackett walk away from IDEO thinking they never had an experience like that in their lives. The answer is that it appeals to the childlike aspirations of all of us to be continually creative.'

The way IDEO stays 'continually creative' is to avoid some of the pitfalls that have befallen other well-known design firms. Most design organizations, according to Kelley, are hierarchical ateliers with an all-powerful design master at the top, supported by apprentices. But issues of consistency, morale and succession eventually undermine this approach. IDEO has deliberately eschewed both the pyramid structure and the star system, organizing the firm into a series of small, guerilla-like operating studios which have no more than around 25 to 30 people in each. Its flat multi-disciplinary 'hot team' structure is democratic, engages the client directly in the work, and reflects the idea that 'big ideas come from small teams'. Each studio has a high degree of autonomy: it can design its own space and determine its own direction according to its needs and interests, free of rules from the centre.

Anarchy is avoided by a governing mechanism known as the 'round table', which meets regularly to form a senior IDEO management group. It is presided over by David Kelley. Each studio has two seats at the round table – one for the studio's creative head, one for its operational head. That makes 24 people sitting at the round table, plus Kelley. Additional people 'bring food and water to the table' on specific issues, according to Kelley. 'This is a very different approach to top-down management. It gives maximum autonomy to the individual studios.'

The extent of this autonomy quickly becomes clear when you visit the different studios, each of which is highly individual. Even before its tie-up with Steelcase, IDEO was already experimenting with alternative workplace design in recognition of the symbiotic relationship between culture, behaviour and habitat. The IDEO team in San Francisco, for example, is sited in an old, characterful waterfront warehouse with spectacular views across the bay. Its large, open space is flexibly organized to allow the users to reconfigure their environment to suit the changing demands of a project, with a 'Wing' to house the studio and a 'Wall' to provide defined client areas.

The Tokyo office is as compact as San Francisco is expansive. Designed on the 'hoteling principle' to give visiting IDEO staffers a temporary home in Japan, it utilizes special translucent mobile furniture elements to make the most of limited space. The London office is different again: a large, airy, industrial-looking building designed with a glass frontage open to the thriving Clerkenwell creative district of the city. Even IDEO's studios along one street in Palo Alto have distinct personalities: at different points you will be greeted by giant hanging velvet drapes or white cubes or shelves of robotic toys or bicycles suspended on ropes from the ceiling or upturned umbrellas to deflect light from the computers. 'One team told me they needed to spend $4,000 on a DC3 aeroplane wing to hang up in their studio,' recalls Kelley with a shrug. 'The general principle with work environments at IDEO is to try stuff and then ask for forgiveness, rather than ask for permission first.'

A Monday morning meeting at IDEO where the week starts with a show-and-tell for all staff.

IDEO staffers stand in the fountain at Trafalgar Square, London.

Little wonder that business guru Tom Peters wrote in Forbes magazine that as soon as you walk into IDEO's Palo Alto headquarters, 'you'll be caught up in the energy, buzz, creative disarray and sheer lunacy of it all.' According to Peters: 'IDEO is a zoo.... Experts of all flavors commingle in "offices" that look more like cacophonous kindergarten classrooms.... Brainstorming sessions, pitting a dozen minds from different disciplines against one another in raucous pursuit of zany ideas, are called on at a moment's notice.'

Peters is on record as saying that of all the companies he has ever looked at and written about, 'IDEO is the only one where I'd love to work'. But getting a job at IDEO can be difficult. The firm is painstaking in its recruitment process to ensure the right fit between applicants and its team culture. Send in your curriculum vitae and you can expect to be interviewed several times and vetted over lunch by up to ten IDEO staffers. Many well-qualified designers have been rejected by IDEO, not because they weren't competent or talented enough, but because they lacked the intellectual curiosity IDEO is always looking for.

Curious intellects always willing to take on new challenges and immerse themselves in new problems contribute to a work culture of punishingly long hours – 50 to 60 hours a week are not uncommon at IDEO. The firm isn't big on official titles or formal promotions. It encourages higher standards of performance mainly through peer pressure and a bizarre ritual of internal prizes and trophies. As one designer remarked,'The only way to enhance your reputation in the organization is by earning the respect of your peers.' In place of hierarchy, there are mentors. David Kelley is at pains to point out that although there may sometimes appear to be chaos during the innovation process, 'it is focused chaos'.

Each IDEO studio starts the week with a show-and-tell Monday morning meeting attended by every member of staff. This isn't a stuffy, minuted affair at a boardroom table but a large, often noisy gathering at which models and concepts are shown, ideas are floated and information exchanged. Each IDEO studio also subscribes to a set of underlying principles known as FLOSS: F stands for Failure, meaning don't be afraid to take risks; L stands for Left-handed – remember that not all users are like you; O stands for Out there – don't just sit at your desk; S stands for Sloppy – prototypes don't need to be perfect; and the final S for Stupid – don't try to be too clever or presume you know it all.

The general principle with work environments is to try stuff and then ask for forgiveness

This simple philosophy finds expression during a five-step innovation process which IDEO has patented as its own: Understand; Observe; Visualize; Evaluate; and Implement. Each project stage holds up a mirror to IDEO's special culture and environment. The Understand phase of any project kicks off with team meetings and brainstorms which aim to get a handle on the problem and get inside the minds of potential users of a product. This stage is all about grasping the business, marketing and technical issues at the heart of the project, about setting out initial insights and product ideas that can be fleshed out later. Who are the competitors? Who are the customers? What technologies can be utilized? What profit margin does the client want to achieve? What is the lifecycle of the product? This first phase also enables the IDEO team to work out which users should be observed.

The second phase – Observe – entails getting 'out there' to conduct observation studies of existing and potential users of the product. Initially IDEO sent out cognitive psychologists to do this work alone and report back to the designers in the studio. Now joint teams of designers and human scientists undertake assignments. 'This enables designers to build empathy with users on site and start thinking creatively about how they can improve things,' explains David Kelley. From the information gathered, user profiles and usability requirements are created and functional specifications defined.

At the Monday morning meeting, everyone is encouraged to share knowledge, talk and interact. 'Hot teams' in a flat organizational structure are valued over hierarchies and titles.

In this phase, IDEO tries to study those it describes as lead users or early adopters. If it is developing a new soft drink bottle, for example, it will observe people who either never buy soft drinks or consume more than 20 a week, not the mass of users in the middle. IDEO has pioneered the use of many forms of non-interventionist observation in its practice, including video ethnography, in order to really understand how people behave. According to Tom Kelley, IDEO's general manager and brother of David, 'Traditional market research asks people questions about what they do and the design is based on what they say. But there is a difference between what they say they do and what they really do. IDEO observational research deals with what people are really doing and feeling.' Tom Kelley believes this distinction is particularly important in the IT industry where male users having a hard time with new software, for example, are notoriously reluctant to admit they are experiencing any problem.

The third step of the process – Visualize – is where industrial design really shines. IDEO develops detailed scenarios in the form of storyboards or videos showing how people might use a product or service, and creates physical models and rough working prototypes to elicit feedback. Fictional characters are invented with real names, personalities, jobs, hobbies, passions and phobias that everyone can relate to. These are adopted by designers during a narrative storytelling process which stimulates rapid-fire design ideas. The most promising of these ideas are swiftly translated into rough 3D models you can touch and hold, which are valued much more highly than 2D sketches. 'We build lots and lots of imperfect prototypes, not because we think we've got the right answer, but to get responses from buyers and users,' explains David Kelley. 'Then we can respond to their comments and fix their complaints. Our design process is like a spiral. We're into multiple realizations of what the future can be.'

'Faking the future', as David Kelley describes the rough-and-ready IDEO formula of building lots of crude prototypes, is quite unlike the traditional design process of presenting the client with just one or two polished 'expert' solutions. But Kelley believes there are powerful advantages to the 'fast, fearless prototyping' that he demands from IDEO designers. 'Take an example like new kitchen appliances. If you just provide a written report on new voice-activated appliances, the client can take it or leave it. But if you actually build tomorrow's kitchen, they can walk right in, experience it and take a view. You can get people to think in a new mode.'

He recalls the senior executives of Whirlpool, a large American appliance manufacturer, standing in a specially mocked-up 'kitchen of the future' at IDEO. Voice-activated refrigerators and washing machines appeared to respond to their spoken commands. 'Open door' was the shouted instruction and the machine behaved accordingly. The technology didn't actually work of course – the future had been faked. Designers hid behind the appliances, operating them manually. But the scenario demonstrated the creative possibilities of new technology far more vividly than any report or design sketches ever could – and it provided valuable information for the Whirlpool management team to make decisions about innovation. That is a typical example of IDEO's Visualize stage in action and there are many others, some very unpolished indeed. The initial prototype for the first Apple mouse, for example, was a butter dish with parts glued inside to hold the rolling ball.

Design visualizations and predictions of this kind help to change people's mindsets and are central to making companies behave in a more innovative way, believes David Kelley, who claims that neither conventional management consultancy nor traditional design methods can achieve this kind of reach. Leading academics such as Robert Sutton, Professor of Organizational Behaviour at Stanford University, tend to agree. 'People at IDEO believe the road to success is paved with constant failure and the lessons that failure reveals,' says Sutton. In the London office, IDEO ergonomist Alison Black observes that 'our studios are cluttered with "the ones we made earlier", a testimony to our policy of trial many times to succeed once'.

The fourth step in the process – Evaluate – enables the development team to review options and refine the working design. Often this involves going back to the user groups observed at stage two for their comments, as well as undertaking lab and field tests. Up to this point, the development has been entirely user-centred – one of IDEO's great strengths, according to David Kelley. But with the onset of the fifth and final stage – Implement, the phase of engineering design and manufacture – the project returns again to the viewpoint of the client. As Kelley explains: 'We may have designed a superb range of home office furniture from a user's point of view, but here we look again at whether the client should be producing it and whether the right distribution is in place.'

IDEO model shop in Palo Alto: the emphasis is on building 3D prototypes that people can respond to as part of an iterative development process.

Interior view of the San Francisco office shows flexible public area used for a wide range of work tasks and events. IDEO invests in making its environments different.

Once the business decision has been made, then the detailed design work for production is done. The Implement phase takes up 90 per cent of the cost and time of any project, according to IDEO. 'Most companies conduct market research, do a small degree of visualization and then implement. What is missing is the user-based observation, evaluation and refinement using rapid prototyping,' believes Kelley.

IDEO puts great emphasis on strong, well-documented implementation which maintains the design integrity by referring back to initial user requirements. It is the only way, says Kelley, to avoid the unrealizable solutions that industrial designers were once notorious for foisting on clients. He accepts that 'the whole world is focused on implementation, on circles of quality, on technologies and manufacturing. But we have shown that if you are confident and informed about implementation, you can also put a recognized methodology on the fuzzy front end of the design process.'

That ability to bottle the creative 'fuzzy front end' and sell it back to large companies is a hallmark of IDEO. One of the ways the firm does this is via an extensive innovation masterclass for clients, entitled IDEO U (the U stands for University). Senior executives from such corporations as BT, Nestlé, Samsung and BMW pay for the privilege of being part of the action on the IDEO campus for up to three months at a time. In addition, senior designers from client companies join IDEO teams on secondment. According to Tom Peters, 'I don't know of anyone else as focused on transferring their own product design knowledge and processes to another organization.'

In doing all this, IDEO is not just creating a new revenue stream as a design consulting firm, but is championing the role of design in industry. As Chee Pearlman, former editor-in-chief of ID Magazine, America's most influential design journal, has observed: 'By transferring the process of innovation to clients, IDEO is in the position to help design become a more important part of our culture.' This culture of transfer and of sharing knowledge works within IDEO itself. Kelley describes project work as 'a lot like making a movie. You pick the best, assemble a team, work intensely for a few months and then disband. Depending on the project, there may be a scramble of people moving from one office to another. Other times, people in different cities work together via conferencing, e-mail or our intranet.' The firm also has a personnel policy that facilitates job-swaps for up to a year between designers at different IDEO locations.

IDEO takes the idea of knowledge-brokering, based on learning from each project, very seriously indeed. This is evident from a resource it has developed for its teams and clients called the Tech Box. Curated by senior engineers Dennis Boyle and Rickson Sun, this is a unique collection of new materials, mechanisms and technologies which serves as the firm's collective creative memory when new innovation challenges arise. Inside a series of black cabinets, the black art of the product developer is revealed – from tiny motors smaller than a pin to memory metals that perform like a human muscle.

The Tech Box is the design engineer's equivalent of the artist's palette and it is constantly being updated with 'cool new things' according to Rickson Sun. In its physical incarnation, it receives a steady stream of visitors, but since 1997 it has also been available online in expanded form right across the firm's international network via IDEO's intranet system. In select cases, clients are given access to a resource which Dennis Boyle describes as the 'crown jewels' of IDEO's innovation process.

Many firms might baulk at the degree of openness with which IDEO conducts its business. In sharing its knowledge and process so readily, it could be argued that IDEO is in danger of passing its expertise so far into the public realm that over time it could render itself obsolete. In practice, however, the opposite has happened during its first decade in business. The more IDEO has opened itself up to the industrial world, the greater the clamour from clients to be part of its special culture and environment.

Our design process is like a spiral. We're into multiple realizations of what the future can be

When IDEO was chosen as Design Team of the Year in 1996 by Design Zentrum Nordrhein Westfahlen in Essen, Germany, an exhibition of the firm's work was created featuring an interactive 'brainstorm' wall. Bill Moggridge is shown (right) scribing at the wall. Around the room, continuous images were projected and a soundtrack was broadcast of IDEO teams at work in five international cities.

IDEO

IDEO Product Development dankt
Samsung Electronics &
ORAL-B Laboratories

vehr herzlich für ihre Unterstützung

www.IDEOeurope.com

IDEO Product Development
3 Jeffreys Place
Jeffreys Street
London
NW1 9PP
ENGLAND

Tel: +44 171 485 1170
Fax: +44 171 482 3976

radius,
Wanderpokal
für das Design-Team des Jahres
Material: Zinn

Design: Simon Peter Eiber,
Weinstadt-Schnait

gesponsert von der Firma
Gebr. Niessing GmbH & Co., Vreden

The evidence of creative brainstorming at the Palo Alto office in northern California. Rules about encouraging wild ideas, deferring judgement and building on the ideas of others are part of IDEO's Post-it note culture.

In IDEO's Palo Alto office, cycles are suspended from the ceiling, a reflection of individual autonomy and control over the work environment. David Kelley explains that the general principle is try out new ideas and then ask for forgiveness, rather than ask for permission first.

View of IDEO at work in
Palo Alto offices, California.
New project rooms are
created as necessary
and brainstorm notes are
witness to the creative
energy generated by
a focus on developing a
different culture and
environment.

A typical IDEO work area in Palo Alto, filled with inspirational materials and collections of toys and objects that aim to stimulate the IDEO designers and engineers who come into contact with them every day.

IDEO studio views on the firm's Palo Alto campus. The suspended aeroplane wing is a prized possession. A group of designers went to a graveyard for planes, fell for an old DC3 wing and brought it back to be displayed in the studio. David Kelley decided that $4,000 was a reasonable price to pay to create an innovative environment, the principle being to experiment and then ask for forgiveness, rather than ask for permission.

IDEO founder David Kelley takes centre-floor position for a Monday morning meeting. Getting everything out in the open and encouraging debate is central to IDEO's teamworking philosophy, but not everyone suits the oddball organizational dynamic and the relentless intellectual curiosity.

Recruitment is therefore an arduous process, as IDEO takes great pains to ensure the right fit between applicants and its team culture.

The reception area at the San Francisco office, which is based in a waterfront warehouse by the Bay Bridge. One of IDEO's most spectacular environments, it is a flexible, airy and dynamic space with great views over the water.

The Tech Box, IDEO's special collection of cool new materials, mechanisms and technologies. It is collated from experience gained by working for clients across more than 40 industries. IDEO's organizational memory resides in the Tech Box, which is also available online across IDEO's intranet system, as Tech Box creator Dennis Boyle (right) demonstrates.

Every year a 'soapbox' race is organized on the Sand Hill Road in Palo Alto, home of many venture capital companies in Silicon Valley. Teams are invited to enter the Sand Hill Challenge with their own improvised vehicle to compete for the fastest time. In 1999 an IDEO team entered the race with a mechanized dragon. Great fun was had by all. The Sand Hill Challenge is just one example of IDEO's emphasis on teambuilding via the zany, offbeat ritual of competitions, prizes and trophies.

They see a broader palette of technologies and design solutions than any other design firm. They just have their fingers in many more pies

Professor Robert Sutton, Stanford University

Detail of Leap Chair for Steelcase. A breakthrough in seating technology, protected by 23 patents. Following its debut, Leap generated record-setting pre-production orders, as well as exceptional publicity for Steelcase.

Bruce Nussbaum, a senior editor at Business Week, coined the term; IDEO helped to create the mindset. 'Product lust' applies to those things 'you just have to have', according to IDEO's David Kelley. In its short ten-year history, IDEO has designed a mini-mountain of products that have successfully gone into production: palmtop computers, toy guitars, toothbrushes, personal digital assistants, ski goggles, car audio equipment, office furniture, microwave ovens, mobile phones, dental equipment, cameras and printers have all originated from the IDEO fun factory to underline the firm's status as designers for industry.

Few areas of business have been untouched by IDEO's influence, from medical and marine to automotive, appliances and IT. The firm even played a role in the Pepsi versus Coca-Cola wars, developing a new Twist 'n Go take-out cup to enable Pepsi to compete more effectively with Coke in the soda fountain trade centred on restaurants and movie theatres.

IDEO may have sold many international clients on its five-step innovation process, but its founders claim that the organization has always been much more interested in content than process. 'We don't care if we sometimes go down the wrong routes, so long as we eventually arrive at the right product,' emphasizes Kelley. Getting it right in the end matters a lot to IDEO. Developing a product that can be manufactured and marketed successfully is not just a testament to its skills in implementation – a traditional design consulting weakness – but reflects well on the entire creative process. And the more projects that are taken into production, the more experienced and knowledgeable IDEO becomes in developing artefacts that either create new markets or redefine existing ones.

Robert Sutton, Professor of Organizational Behaviour at Stanford University, sees economies of scale in such an accumulative approach to product development. 'IDEO is routinely creative because it's a knowledge broker,' explains Sutton. 'Just because they're the biggest and work with a wide array of industries, they see a broader palette of technologies and design solutions than any other design firm. They just have their fingers in many more pies.'

Even before IDEO's formation, there were business stories to write home about: David Kelley Design's Microsoft Mouse, for example, sold more than 7 million units in a single year. And once the firm was up and running, there were new measures of design effectiveness. The Neat Squeeze toothpaste dispenser for Proctor & Gamble, for example, captured 5 per cent of a $1 billion market in its first year following launch. The first in a series of new-look computer products for NEC, the Versa, doubled NEC's market share of notebook computers in the US in just six months. A redesign of Ford's own brand of audio equipment, offered as an option with each Ford car, saw the numbers of Ford customers choosing to keep the equipment shoot up from 13 to 97 per cent. A computer keyboard support designed for Details, a division of Steelcase, sold $40 million worth of product in its first year. And a cellular flip phone for the Mercury One-2-One network in the UK, manufactured by Motorola, was so popular in the three months following its launch in September 1993, that Mercury exhausted its entire inventory.

We don't care if we sometimes go down the wrong routes, so long as we arrive at the right product

Quadlux Flashbake Oven, which uses banks of halogen lightbulbs to cook food more rapidly than a conventional oven. Unlike microwaves, the wide light spectrum of halogen bulbs cooks food with heat and deeply penetrating infrared rays, allowing chefs to brown meat and baked goods. The design recognizes this oven as a professional and high-technology tool; it uses formed stainless steel for the door and bezel to avoid the flat, featureless look of microwave ovens.

In every case, the hot-selling product in question was designed with features that really appealed to user needs – and these user needs were identified, investigated and validated during the stages of understanding, observing and visualizing. Not surprisingly, given the commercial impact of so many IDEO projects, its process has been scrutinized by the US business schools to find the magic formula. Attention has focused in particular on the twin engines of innovation at IDEO, creative brainstorming and continuous prototyping. According to David Kelley, 'Brainstorming mines the intellectual raw materials; prototyping shapes them into something that can be communicated, demonstrated, tested and improved. The two work best in rapid-fire sequence.'

Robert Sutton and fellow academic Andrew Hargadon of Stanford University conducted a 15-month ethnographic study of IDEO brainstorming techniques. Their conclusions (published by Cornell University in December 1996) challenged existing research that face-to-face brainstorming sessions are inefficient compared to working alone. They discovered that brainstorming 'supports organizational memory' by helping IDEO designers to acquire, store, retrieve, adapt and combine knowledge of potential solutions in order to design products, and 'provides skill variety' by enabling designers to stretch and learn from a wide range of experts and techniques. Brainstorming also supports 'an attitude of wisdom' in that IDEO designers are not over-cautious or over-confident but reflect and reinforce organizational values by asking others in the team for help and by getting a range of opinions and views on any subject.

This concept of 'an attitude of wisdom' – which was first used in academic writing in 1990 to describe a person who acts with knowledge while simultaneously doubting what he or she knows – is very helpful in understanding IDEO's track record of design for industry. There is, suggest Sutton and Hargadon, a constructive humility inherent in its creative brainstorming process, which enables market-friendly products to emerge at the end of it.

Another US academic, Michael Schrage of the MIT Sloan School of Management, studied IDEO's commitment to the working prototype. In a paper published in Design Management Journal (winter 1993), Schrage quoted David Kelley as saying 'I strongly believe that prototypes and products are intimately related, that the number of prototypes and quality of those prototypes is directly proportional to the ultimate quality of the product.' Schrage's argument was that prototypes are not simply useful models that map out a product's specification, but are indicators of a company's overall ability to innovate. He concluded that 'remaking our prototypes may enable us to remake our organizations'. In this context, IDEO's powerful emphasis on continuous prototyping may give it an edge when developing products that will be confidently invested in and backed to the hilt by the company.

David Kelley and Bill Moggridge both recognize that the higher up you go in any manufacturing company, the harder it becomes for executives to visualize what the new product will be like. That is why developing prototypes and models that 'fake the future' are so helpful. IDEO's leaders recognize too that different industries innovate at different speeds according to their characteristics. Competitive pressures in the car and computer industries, for example, turn the innovation wheels ever faster, whereas the monoliths of medical equipment, furniture and appliances tend to move at a slower rate. But even in areas where the design pace is hot, IDEO's focus on narrative storytelling with invented characters to reveal user motivation has been effective in suggesting new directions.

'The car industry is smarter than most at designing for users,' says Kelley. 'But even in the automotive industry, tricks can be missed. We heard that Dodge pick-up trucks did some work to find out what users really want. The company thought their vehicles were being driven by rednecks, cowboys. They discovered the real users were small businessmen who needed multiple cigarette lighter sockets to recharge the mobile phone and laptop computer.'

A constructive humility creates market-friendly products

Dishwasher for LG Electronics, one of a trio of future appliances designed as part of a 'Kitcheneering' project.

The Brivo Box, for Brivo Systems Inc., uses internet technology for delivery of online ordering. A further example of IDEO's use of new technologies in the development of products for the market.

IDEO's work on a handheld charger for electrically powered vehicles for Hughes Power Control Systems, a division of General Motors, further illustrates the importance of the user narrative. By investigating a range of user behaviours, IDEO designers and human factors specialists decided that four different types of charger were required by users: not just a 110 volt adaptor handheld unit for storing in the vehicle itself, but also a 220 volt wall-mounted residential module, a 220 volt curbside column and a kiosk-style energy station for powering up the vehicle. Design scenarios envisaged users parking their electric commuter vehicle at an energy station and letting it charge for the day while they take the light rail to the office (the first actual installation was at Walnut Creek, California).

The character portraits in the scenarios were instrumental in determining what form the charger should take. Here's one: 'Kilo, 51 years old, married to Otto. No children. Two cats. Lives in Sausalito Hills. Old shingled detached home with small yard. Has own nature travel and adventure business. Democrat. Husband repairs old boats. Likes birdwatching and whalewatching. Supports the symphony. Purchased her EV (Electric Vehicle) when her six-year-old Honda was stolen. Pleased to have option of clean, quiet car – but uninterested in what happens under the hood.'

Championing the user has also been effective for IDEO in the computer industry, where the tendency has been to become fixated by technologies advancing so rapidly that they often outstrip the capacity of people to understand them. 'Recent trends have clearly worked to our advantage,' explains David Kelley, 'in that things are now moving so fast that it makes much more sense to study the human user than to study technology.' When, for example, IDEO worked on the award-winning Palm V electronic organizer, manufactured by Palm Computing, the project was codenamed 'razor' to reflect the desire to develop a thin-as-a-razor product that could go easily into a pocket or purse and therefore appeal to women.

15 female IDEO staffers critiqued the company's existing chunky Palm Pilot during development in order to create a sleeker, slimmer product; and lead engineer Dennis Boyle collected an array of elegant Japanese gadgets to indicate the level of finesse required. The resulting Palm V is an ultra-thin (and ultra-cool) design which has wowed Silicon Valley, but it took a full year before Palm's manufacturers in Utah, Texas, California and Asia could produce the anodized aluminium casing to the super-slim dimensions specified by IDEO.

On another electronic project, for internet publisher SoftBook Press, IDEO developed the SoftBook in recognition of the fact that users still generally prefer getting information from books than from computer screens. The SoftBook is a device that has a built-in modem, plugs directly into a phone line and holds up to 100,000 pages of content. But its portrait-style page makes its screen unlike that of any computer or TV, and it downloads information a page at a time like a book to avoid awkward computer-scrolling through documents. A comfortable wedge shape for reading and a leather cover help to reinforce the book metaphor.

In the age of the internet, IDEO has shaped a new generation of web-based appliances, not because it is in love with the worldwide web, but because it takes the time to explore how people want to interact with it. The firm deliberately designed the Audible MobilePlayer – which enables users to listen to audio material downloaded from the internet even when they are in the gym or on the beach – to look unlike portable CD and cassette players. The metaphor is the human ear, with the all-important play button at the centre of the nautilus shape. The manufacturer is New Jersey start-up Audible Inc.

It makes more sense to study the human user than to study technology

The story of technology push versus user pull is even more pronounced in the office furniture industry, which manages to make the IT sector look positively user-focused in comparison. The scientifically managed corporate workplace over the past 100 years has been notorious for putting the technology-driven needs of management efficiency above the human needs of individuals. Office workers are rarely 'consumers' of the products they use at work in the conventional sense, and are often alienated from any design process. In this context, IDEO's work with its investment partner Steelcase Inc. in exploring more vividly and creatively the world of the office user has been an eye-opener within an industry dominated by three or four big players.

Several leading-edge products have emerged from the relationship. These include Steelcase's Pathways office system, for which IDEO led the engineering development, and the Leap Chair, which incorporates advanced ergonomics as a powerful market response to rival Herman Miller's popular Aeron model. For Steelcase subsidiary Vecta, IDEO designed a task chair that stacks called Kart – as the designers discovered, it was no easy task to combine a high level of comfort with the requirement to flip up for storage.

In Europe, where Steelcase also has a sizeable presence, IDEO developed a flexible new furniture system called 1 + 1. Aimed at the entire European market, this was designed with common components to offer the widest possible range of configurations, so that the system could be tailored to the cultural needs of users in different European countries. Its key element is an extruded aluminium rail, onto which legs and tabletops are attached, enabling a huge variety of shapes and sizes. At least some of the thinking that informed the design of 1+1 derived from an advanced study of the behaviour of mobile workers, entitled Moving, which IDEO London and Steelcase jointly undertook. Storyboarding and scenario-building revealed first, the need for rapid-response reconfiguration of work settings, and second, workspaces which support company learning. Both ideas were expressed in the development of Steelcase's 1+1 product range.

However, it is in the relatively slow-moving medical equipment industry where IDEO's design-for-market credentials perhaps shine most brightly. Here is a sector that traditionally put technical and clinical needs ahead of the user experience. Take eyetests for detection of glaucoma, for example. Patients had to endure putting their head inside a large, noisy metal box with blinking lights for up to 40 minutes. The process was 'out of the Spanish Inquisition', according to medical device-maker Humphrey Instruments, which teamed up with IDEO to develop a more user-friendly alternative. The Field Analyser 11 has a curvilinear form and large, easy-to-press buttons, which makes things a lot easier for patients, especially older ones, who predominate on glaucoma eyetests.

A similar story can be told in dental equipment. Nobody likes going to the dentist, but IDEO was determined to improve things for the patient. Its designers worked on a new AirTouch cavity detection and treatment system with Midwest Dental, transforming a formerly cumbersome and terrifying toolset into a modern, non-intimidating robot-cabinet. The AirTouch process itself uses a combination of aluminium oxide particles and pressured air to remove decay more quickly and with less pain.

Other IDEO medical innovations show similar advances – from a nifty portable heart pump developed with Baxter Healthcare, which has transformed the emergency treatment of heart failure patients, to a clever disposable insulin injection device for Eli Lilly, which allows users to carry insulin for up to 28 days without refrigeration. In the medical area, maybe it is not so much 'product lust' as 'product lifeline'. But like producers everywhere, medical manufacturers also have to meet market needs, out-innovate competitors and turn a profit. So perhaps the last word here should belong to Bruce Nussbaum, who wrote in <u>Business Week</u>: 'Design equals the bottom line…. It's not about pretty shapes, but about the function of those shapes. It's not about technology per se, but about how high tech is applied through the product for the consumer's use.'

Design is not about pretty shapes but about function

Audible MobilePlayer, developed for Audible Inc., is a handheld storage and playback system that uses sophisticated audio compression technology to transfer spoken books and speeches from the internet. It enables users to listen to audio material downloaded from the internet even when they are in the gym or on the beach. Its design is based on the metaphor of the human ear, with the all-important play button at the centre of the nautilus shape.

The Palm V electronic organizer, made by 3Com, is a sleek, elegant product, half the thickness of the original PalmPilot, with an anodized aluminium housing and an internal lithium ion battery. The development project was codenamed 'razor' to reflect the desire to develop a thin-as-a-razor product that could go easily into a pocket or purse and therefore appeal to women users.

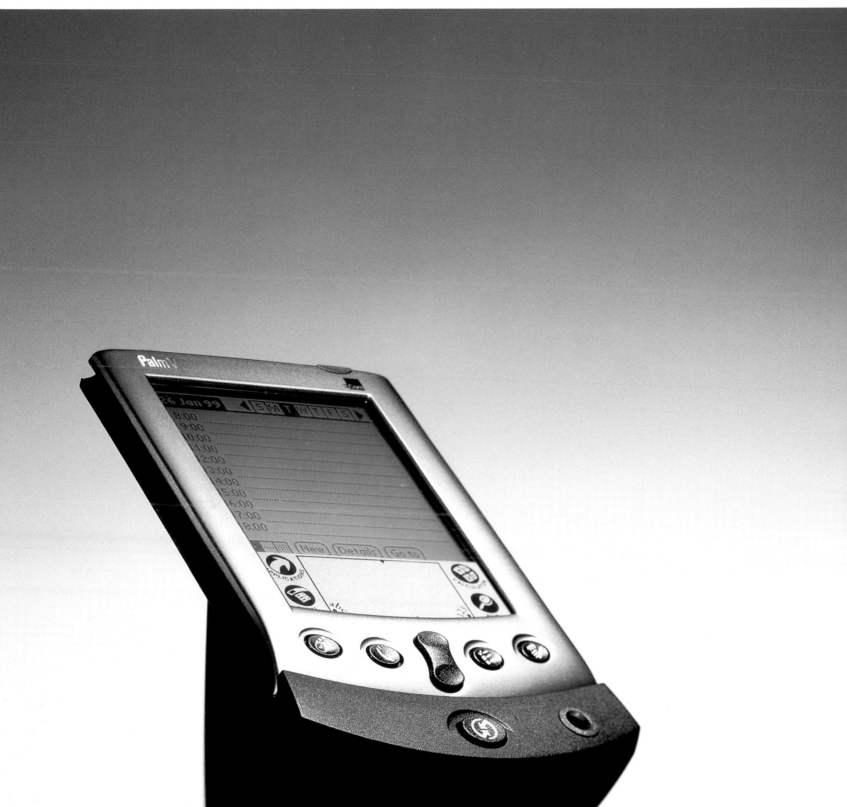

New Generation fishing
kits designed for Berkley:
a package to provide
everything for the
enthusiastic first-time
fisherman, including bait,
tackle and line.

Flashcast SP2000
Integrated Spin Reel:
a low-cost, spin-casting
rod/reel to simplify the
fishing experience and
optimize user comfort.
It was winner of a silver
design award from
Business Week in 1995.

Sentry medical system, designed for Bridge Medical. It delivers multiple intravenous drugs at a patient's bedside. The needs of the patient, the caregiver, the hospital and the pharmacist were carefully considered during this product's development.

Humalog/Humulin Insulin Pen, developed with medical manufacturer Eli Lilly. The first disposable insulin pen to offer single-unit doses. Simple and easy to use, it enables users to carry insulin for up to 28 days without refrigeration, thus allowing them to maintain an active lifestyle.

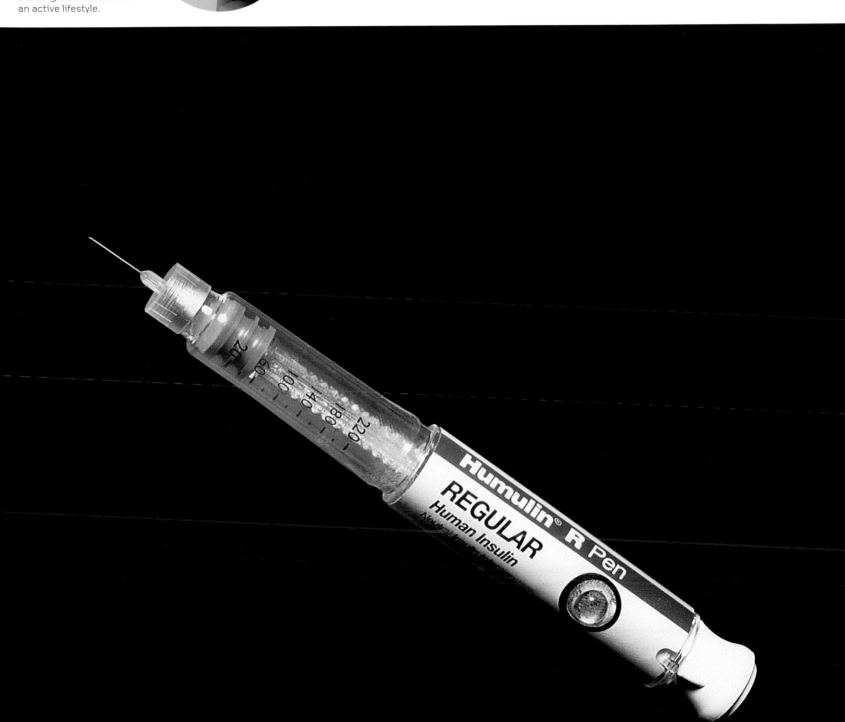

Cisco IP Phone signals
a new direction in
communication technology
without additional
complexity. Incorporation
of the IP telephone system
extends the functionality
of internet technology
by allowing voice and data
to travel over the same
network infrastructure.

A joint project with Hughes Power Control Systems, a division of General Motors, to develop a handheld charger for electrically powered vehicles. Scenarios of potential users were created to put the products into the context of real people's lives and a series of chargers were designed for different environments.

Shown here (clockwise): a charging unit for the private garage; a large charging unit for public spaces; a charging unit and payment system for public use such as car parks at railway stations and shopping malls; user scenarios; and a paddle for charging.

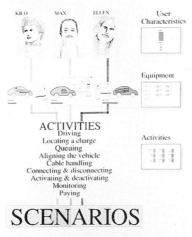

ACTIVITIES
Driving
Locating a charge
Queuing
Aligning the vehicle
Cable handling
Connecting & disconnecting
Activating & deactivating
Monitoring
Paying

SCENARIOS

Ellen

Gender   Female
Age   33
Marital status Single
Children   None
Pets   None
Location of home Portola Valley, rented in-law house.
Car Storage   Carport, off street

Occupation   Business consultant. She is self-employed and works from home.
                Most of her clients are in silicon valley. MBA Stanford.

Lifestyle   Skis winters at Squaw Valley. She plays tennis and likes to ride
                bikes with a group of friends. She would like to buy a house and
                have a family but hasn't decided when.

Personality   Everything is her passion. She hates wasting time. She is an over-
                achiever and knows it.

Spouse   Not married. Dating a man who likes to have fun is always trying
                to get her to take time off. She is also dating a successful busi-
                ness man who owns a small company that manufactures scientific
                equipment.

Why an EV   She likes the image of being on the cutting edge, because many of
                her clients are in high-tech businesses. She likes the fact that her
                car is from Detroit and is the most advanced technologically.

Use   Intensive infrequent use. She tries to arrange client visits on two
                days per week to consolidate trips in the car because she hates
                wasting time in traffic.

The Ergo Audrey for 3Com
presents a PalmPilot for
the whole family. The clear
antenna in the centre lights
up when you have mail and
doubles as a stylus for the
touchscreen. The device
also syncs with individual
Palms via a cradle.

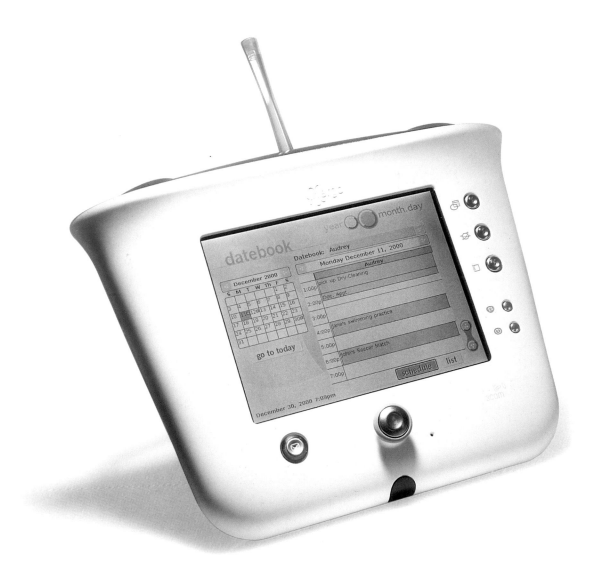

The SoftBook, developed for internet publisher SoftBook Press, is a portable electronic book that is designed to be a replacement for textbooks, business or reference books. A connected appliance that allows text to be downloaded from a telephone line via the internet, it presents information a page at a time like a book to avoid awkward computer-scrolling through documents. The book metaphor is reinforced by a comfortable wedge shape for reading and a leather cover.

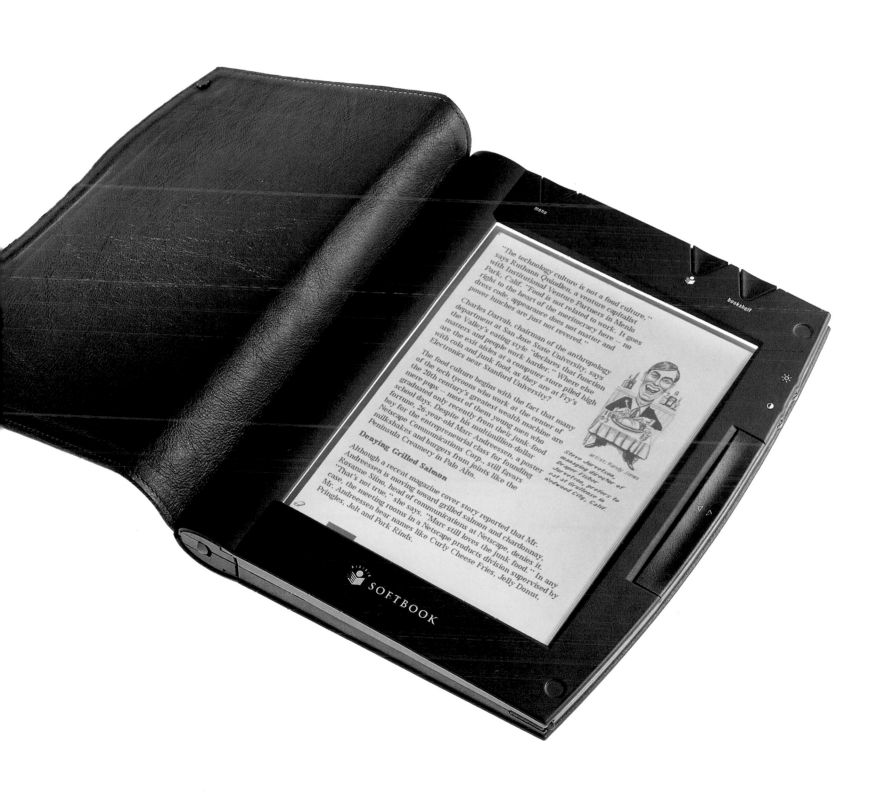

ACCO stapler. The stapler is
usually a mundane piece of
office equipment, but in this
design it is given personality
and appeal by a distinctive
anthropomorphic plastic
hood styling.

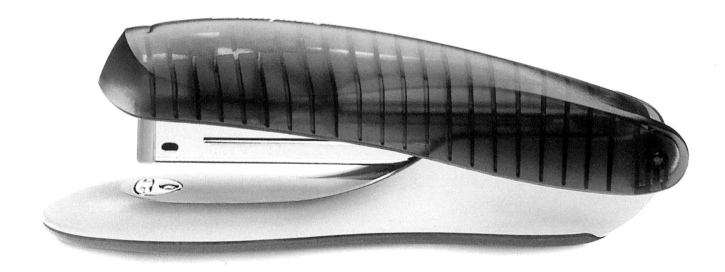

Designed for driving games, Logitech's Wingman Formula Force game controller accurately simulates the look and feel of the Formula One cockpit.

This washing machine
is one of a series of
appliances designed for
LG Electronics as part
of the 'Kitcheneering'
project. A refrigerator
and dishwasher were
designed too. Stainless
steel and rubber bring the
professional kitchen into
the domestic landscape,
making the machine a tool.

One of a range of all-
terrain eyewear for Nike.
The project addressed the
particular issues facing an
athlete wearing sunglasses,
such as fogging, insects
and sweaty skin, by
providing decentred optics
and rubberized nosepieces.
User trials were a key part
of the development process.

068

The CyberMan 2 games controller for Logitech, reflecting the increasingly complex virtual realities of modern computer games. It allows proportional control in the X and Y axes like a conventional mouse, but can also navigate with control in the Z axis, sensing pitch, roll and yaw, to allow the user to move freely in 3D space.

The Home Smart Monitor allows small kitchen appliances to talk to each other through the existing power wiring. IDEO worked with the manufacturer, Merloni, to expand the capabilities of the monitor and increase its connection with daily family life through a family message centre, radio and internet access.

070

Monitors designed for multinational manufacturer NEC take the traditionally bland, boring desktop box in a new direction. The NEC Multimedia Monitor presents a differentiated product image.

The NEC M500 Multi-
Sync Monitor has
sweepingly dramatic lines
that break new ground
in style while providing
seamless integration
of audio and video for
consumer and business
multimedia users.

NEC LT84 Projector, an LCD projector as compact as an A4 file. Unlike any other products of a similar function, it is compact enough to carry without a handle. It is easy to operate in the dark, and the remote control mirrors the layout of the controls on the projector itself.

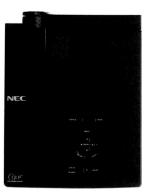

NetSchools' StudyPro Computer: a wireless laptop computer for educational use, aimed at giving educators more flexible methods of teaching, providing internet access, and introducing new technology to each student. Rugged enough to withstand the rigours of daily classroom use, the StudyPro Computer is the cornerstone of the NetSchools system. It was designed as a serious tool, not a toy computer for children. Its magnesium case is protected by colourful shock-absorbing bumpers. A high-speed infrared LAN (Local Area Network) port sits at the top of the display to provide network access from anywhere in the classroom without wires. The keyboard is waterproof, and the unit is easily carried with a large built-in handle.

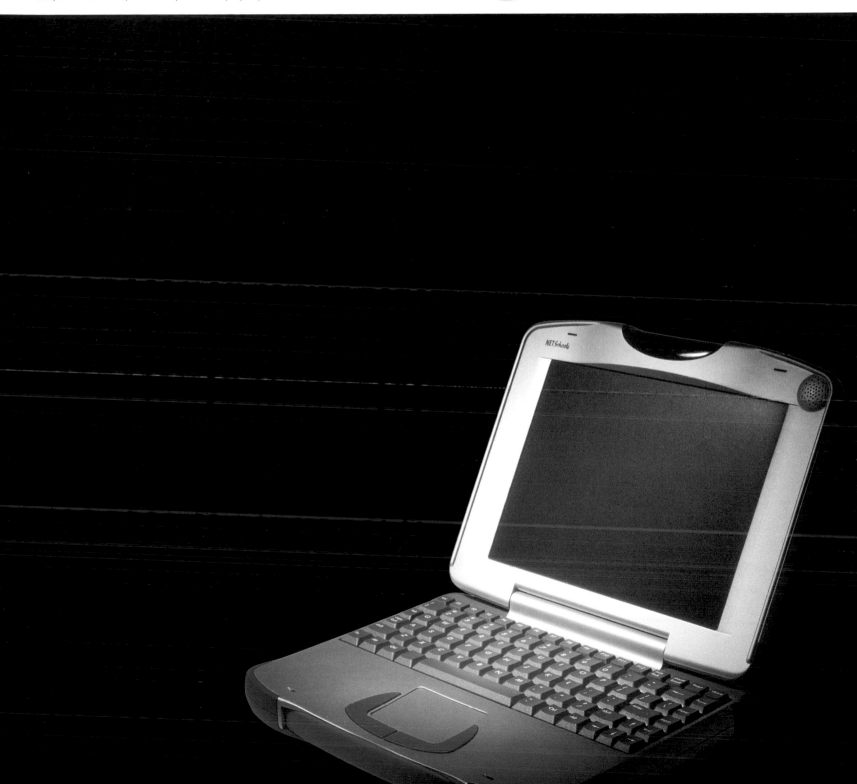

Polaroid's PopShots: the first single-use instant camera. The package encourages the user to return the camera for recycling by including a postage-paid return envelope, a cash refund and a chance to win large prizes. IDEO's multi-disciplinary team of industrial designers, mechanical engineers and human factors specialists adopted an internal architecture that creates a perception of small size, and developed 1-2-3 operational graphics and colour-coded interface features to walk the user through the picture-taking process.

Polaroid's new I-Zone pocket camera creates small instant pictures in seconds, which kids can apply to helmets, books, backpacks and each other, using a special sticky-back film. The I-Zone has become the best-selling camera in the US, adopted by kids from nine to 19. IDEO's human factors and industrial design team spent weeks interviewing the young target market in order to understand their likes and dislikes. By using image boards filled with advertising and recording their tastes in shoes, cameras, watches, personal stereos and computer input devices – all popular purchases in this age group – the team was able to clearly define their preferences. Key to this project was the discovery that children use cameras for 'photo play' – an expression of creativity and a method of connecting with friends.

PRS (Photochemical Recycling System) is a new development that enables photographic fixer solution to be recycled. Hospital X-ray labs present a huge market for this technology. This specially designed unit is moveable between departments without spillage, thus improving safety.

The Psion Wavefinder,
an antenna that allows
PC owners to exploit the
full potential of digital
radio. IDEO was
responsible for industrial
design, interaction design,
branding and naming on
this product development.

3Com Home Connect Cable Modem. A high-speed cable modem for the home with a strong brand message in IDEO's design. The shape is reminiscent of a shark's fin and uses backlit icons and pleasant sounds to indicate activities – a friendly device that does not hide its technological capabilities.

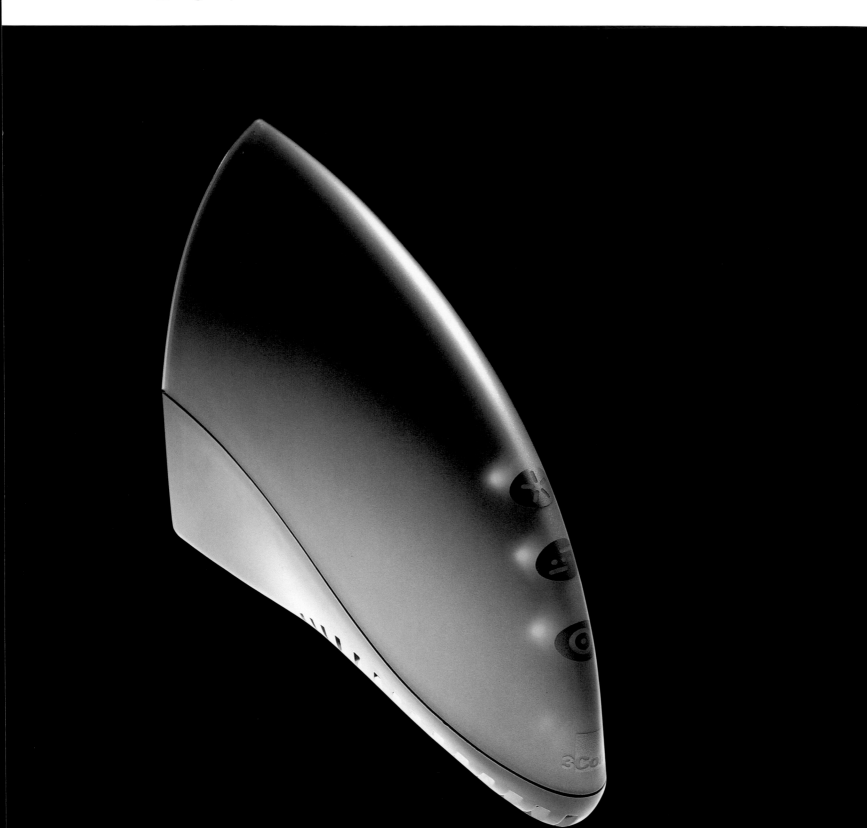

The Steelcase Leap Chair is more than just an adjustable task chair for the office. It represents a significant new technology in back support. Four years of research – 11 studies by 27 scientists at four universities – revealed critical discoveries that guided the design of the chair. IDEO contributed an organic visual language that reveals the chair's elegant mechanics, as well as engineering insights that enabled the original design to be realized in a revolutionary new way. The result is a breakthrough in seating technology, strongly protected by 23 issued and pending patents.

Mobile tables in the Pathways furniture range from Steelcase, a major office system developed and engineered over several years by a joint Steelcase-IDEO team of engineers and designers. Pathways is today one of Steelcase's core systems, its comprehensive family of components capable of creating an entire micro-architecture for the American office.

Details, a Steelcase subsidiary, worked with IDEO to develop this Stella computer keyboard support. A grab-and-place mechanism allows the keyboard to be repositioned without using knobs and other adjustment levers. Through design and engineering, the production cost of this keyboard was reduced by 30 per cent and it proved so successful as a design that it sold $40 million worth of product in its first year.

The 1+1 office furniture system designed by IDEO Europe for Steelcase Strafor. An office system for the European market that accommodates cultural differences across the region and is easily customized for individual preferences and varying office styles. The furniture consists of desk, chairs, cabinets, screens and accessories. IDEO's value engineering process achieved a reduction in manufacturing costs of between 15 per cent and 20 per cent on some components, making the 1+1 system attractive to buyer and seller alike.

The Kart chair, manufactured by Vecta, a Steelcase subsidiary. A joint effort between Vecta, 5D Studio and IDEO, it combines the office task chair with the classic stacking chair. Comfortable and stable enough to be used all day as an office worker's main chair, a flip of the seat allows eight chairs to nest in the space of two and a half. This eases the storage requirements of the facilities manager, who must flexibly arrange corporate training rooms and meeting halls, and provides a better solution for gatherings like classes, seminars and conventions.

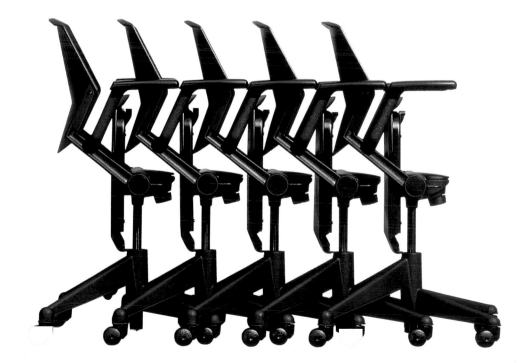

INAX is a Japanese tile and
porcelain manufacturer
which asked IDEO to design
new products for the
bathroom. The Light Tile
(left) emits a soft glow.
The Cup (right) is a storage
tile with a handle.

5 Design the experience

More and more we find ourselves designing complex and dynamic interactions with converging hardware and software, spaces and services

Marion Buchenau and Jane Fulton Suri, IDEO San Francisco

Three examples of 'experience prototyping': IDEO designers and human factors specialists use rough models and methods to understand the process of interaction with our material world and get inside the mind of the user.

In developing products based on the user experience, it was perhaps inevitable that IDEO would venture into designing for what has been described as 'the experience economy'. This aspect of the firm's work has not only involved designing spaces and environments such as showrooms and exhibitions, but also entire user sequences or journeys. IDEO was one of the first design organizations to recognize that certain artefacts, cellphones for example, were increasingly being marketed as services, not as products. That changed the rules of engagement on client projects and allowed the firm's emphasis on the role of human factors research within the design team to come to the fore. As Marion Buchenau and Jane Fulton Suri, two human factors specialists with IDEO San Francisco, explained in a paper entitled 'Experience Prototyping': 'More and more we find ourselves designing complex and dynamic interactions with converging hardware and software, spaces and services – products such as mobile digital communication devices, or systems of connected interactions such as those which occur on a train journey or an internet shopping spree.'

IDEO was thus able to position itself as a designer of interactive systems and experiences, not simply as a stylist or engineer of hardware. It did so initially in a new discipline – interaction design – pioneered by Bill Moggridge in response to the growing interface demands of electronic products. But gradually its focus on framing every step of the user experience permeated its entire approach. In the context of American business practice, this was a significant move. By the late 1990s, the emerging 'experience economy' was becoming a hot topic in management.

In an article in the <u>Harvard Business Review</u> (July–August 1998) entitled 'Welcome to the Experience Economy', two Ohio-based strategic planners, B Joseph Pine II and James H Gilmore, outlined how economies make major gear shifts by charting 'the four stage evolution of the birthday cake'. In the agrarian economy, the authors explained, mothers made birthday cakes from farm commodities such as flour and eggs for just a few dimes. In the industrial economy, they baked cakes using pre-mixed ingredients bought from Betty Crocker for a couple of dollars. In the service economy, they ordered birthday cakes from the bakery or grocery store for $10 to $15. But nowadays, parents no longer make cakes or even buy them in. They don't even host the party. Instead they 'outsource' the entire event to a place such as the Discovery Zone, which is in business to stage parties for kids at $100 a go and which throws in the cake as part of the overall deal. Welcome to the experience economy.

In their Harvard paper, Pine and Gilmore identified Disney as the godfather of the experience economy and gave honourable mentions to others up to a similar game: Nike with its Niketown concept; British Airways with its 'world's favourite airline' focus on the customer; and themed restaurants such as the Hard Rock Café and Planet Hollywood. The authors recognized a major paradigm shift taking place, with key points of differentiation. 'Economists have typically lumped experiences in with services,' they observed, 'but experiences are a distinct economic offering, as different from services as services are from goods.' In terms of economic function, goods are made, services are delivered, but experiences are staged; in terms of the nature of the offering, goods are tangible, services intangible, but experiences are memorable; in terms of user attribute, goods are standardized, services customized, but experiences personal; and in terms of method of supply, goods are inventoried, services delivered on demand, but experiences are revealed over a duration.

Goods are made, but experiences are staged

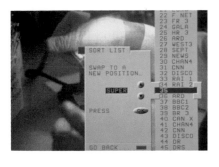

In comparing factors of demand, Pine and Gilmore even went as far as saying that goods have features, services have benefits, but experiences have sensations. This explains why, in a section on how to design memorable experiences, they advised designers to engage all five senses, adding: 'The sensory stimulants that accompany an experience should support and enhance its theme.'

That thinking is central to Bill Moggridge's own philosophy. He believes that, as human beings, we experience designed products, services and spaces through each of the five senses. 'We often call it "beauty with a smile"', he explains. 'Take having a cup of tea, for example. First you look to see if the shape of the cup is beautiful and if the tea inside swirls elegantly. Next, as you lift the cup and bring it to your mouth, you can detect the tea's fragrance. You take a sip. When you return the cup to the saucer, there is a pleasing sound. It is only after going through each of these experiences, from beginning to end, that you appreciate the tea for the first time. This is the experience, and if we can design it successfully, we can satisfy the user – in other words, we can get a smile.'

Moggridge acknowledges that the relatively simple experience of sipping a cup of tea is not an especially challenging one to design. The real challenge comes when you are dealing with the interaction between new technologies and user behaviours. He first recognized the need for a new discipline – termed 'interaction design' – when he was working on the world's first laptop computer, the GRiD Compass, in the early 1980s. He presented his first conference paper on the subject in 1984 and, within two years, he had hired his first interaction design team within Moggridge Associates. To find the people with the hybrid mix of programming, human factors and design skills he needed, Moggridge did a lot of work in education with Stanford University and the Royal College of Art in London to set up the training supply chain.

Moggridge believes that interaction design holds the same position relative to software engineering as industrial design does to mechanical engineering or architectural design does to civil engineering. In other words, it deals with the softer, more subjective, user-based side of the design process as opposed to the harder, more objective, function-driven factors that can more easily be calculated and measured. As a discipline, interaction design allowed IDEO to stage-manage the experience of using an electronic product such as a laptop or mobile phone or digital camera. Expertise in stage-managing memorable experiences was soon the flavour right across the firm's diverse portfolio of projects – even if it meant developing new skills and attitudes within IDEO.

According to Marion Buchenau and Jane Fulton Suri, 'Experience is a very dynamic, complex and subjective phenomenon. It depends on the perception of multiple sensory qualities of a design, interpreted through filters relating to contextual factors.' In their paper 'Experience Prototyping', they explained this using the example of the experience of going down a mountainside on a snowboard: 'It depends on the weight and material qualities of the board, the bindings and your boots, the snow conditions, the weather, the terrain, the temperature of air in your hair, your skill level, your current state of mind, the mood and expression of your companions.'

Buchenau and Fulton Suri concluded: 'The experience of even simple artefacts does not exist in a vacuum but, rather, in dynamic relationship with other people, places and objects.' Quoting a Chinese proverb – 'What I hear, I forget. What I see, I remember. What I do, I understand' – they advocated prototyping methods that allow designers, users and clients to 'experience it themselves', rather than witnessing a demonstration of someone else's experience.

IDEO's work with the US train operator Amtrak to create a new design strategy for a high-speed rail link between Boston and Washington demonstrates much of this new thinking. Amtrak initially talked to IDEO about product innovation associated with the new service. Amtrak was focused on traditional design and engineering specifications, but IDEO quickly identified that a new pasenger experience needed to be designed, not the hardware. As David Kelley recalls, 'It was not about "How beautiful can we make the train interior?" It was about competing with the experience of flying or driving by automobile to Washington. It demanded a different way of thinking.'

Experience is a dynamic, complex and subjective phenomenon

To develop a vision for Amtrak's new service, an IDEO design team based in New York rode Amtrak trains, toured stations, interviewed senior managers, analyzed information distribution, evaluated advertising campaigns and probed customer research. In an example of the 'experience prototyping' discussed by Buchenau and Fulton Suri, they explored different passenger needs through a series of improvised user scenarios, for example buying return tickets from a machine with gloves on or in windy conditions. By analyzing the total passenger experience, IDEO identified ten steps in the 'journey': learning, planning, starting, entering, ticketing, waiting, boarding, riding, arriving and continuing.

Each aspect was then developed in relation to the next as part of a seamless experience. Learning about the Amtrak service via the web or advertising; planning an appropriate schedule with timings and fares; starting out to the rail station with the right information and route and encountering the right baggage handling and car parking services; entering the station with a welcoming infrastructure and environment; ensuring that the ticketing service is well handled; providing platform information, comfort and seating so that waiting is a pleasant drama in anticipation of the train's arrival; boarding the train easily; riding the train with quality onboard business and leisure amenities; providing the right orientation facilities on arrival at the destination; and planning onward journeys for continuing travellers, for example shuttles to conferences – all of these aspects were sewn into a carefully considered passenger narrative.

Amtrak was presented with a set of recommendations and principles that not only added up to an integrated service in operational terms, but also captured the user-friendly spirit of a quality competitor to the airline shuttles between Boston, New York and Washington. These guidelines extended from naming and branding to new trains and station environments, and signalled IDEO's own departure from its orthodox product development roots into the new terrain of designing entire experiences.

IDEO has also gained credibility in environmental design, primarily through a brace of leading-edge Worklife showrooms for Steelcase led by Aura Oslapas in its San Francisco office. The experience of visiting the static displays of most office furniture companies can be a huge yawn. Steelcase wanted its sales environment at Columbus Circle in New York to be a more active resource. IDEO's interviews with staff and customers, and its observational studies, led to the development of creative user scenarios describing typical journeys through the building for different types of customer. Profiles ranged from characters very interested in the physical and material attributes of the furniture to those more focused on intangible issues, such as property costs or downsizing.

An 'experience map' was drawn up to link all possible interactions and this led directly to the spatial planning of the showroom with three main elements: settings, such as a café, mock-up space and meeting space; pods, which present a 'product slice' of each furniture system; and sandboxes, areas which let customers try out different products and materials, and which promote play and active learning. Instead of the showroom staff working in cramped conditions out back, they are based on the floor itself in a range of settings. Following the redesign at Columbus Circle, visitors upped the time spent in the facility from around 40 minutes to nearly two hours per visit and sales climbed by 25 per cent.

Ideas prototyped in New York resurfaced more experimentally in the Steelcase Worklife showroom in Chicago, where visitors were given an 'active badge' to chart their interactions with different media-rich settings within the facility, and where web communications formed part of the sales proposition.

IDEO's environmental expertise, however, is not confined to the USA. IDEO Japan won acclaim in 1998 for an exhibition design for the Miwa Lock Company, which presented a refreshing sense of discovery in the act of using handles to open doors – only to discover more handles. And, in 2000, IDEO London built a Watercycle Pavilion on the site of the Millennium Dome in London's Greenwich. Designed for local utility company Thames Water, this glass structure acted as a window on a sustainable water treatment process which took rainwater from the Dome's giant umbrella roof through 12 hoppers into a natural filtration and recycling system for the site.

All aspects were sewn into a seamless experience

For Bill Moggridge, 'environmental experiences' such as these are the result of a logical progression that has gradually taken the industrial design profession beyond designing for machine and systems behaviour. Moggridge describes this progression as moving from a basic focus on anthropometrics through, successively, physiology, cognitive psychology, sociology and anthropology, towards sustainability. The acknowledged starting point for human factors in design was <u>The Measure of Man</u>, written in 1959 by the American industrial designer Henry Dreyfuss. This established the study of anthropometrics – the dimensions of the human body, including arm and leg reach – as an essential tool for designers; Dreyfuss used standard measures of 'human scale' to determine whether people fitted to designs physically. Once averages had been determined, the mass production doctrine 'one size fits all' applied.

The next step was physiological, the study of how people do things and the testing of physical performance and stresses in relation to design. This was a significant advance and has endured in terms of the idea of design as a problem-solving activity. But as Jane Fulton Suri, who leads the human factors discipline within IDEO, has pointed out, design as problem solving is a limited concept. Fulton Suri explains that for much of the time we are oblivious to the functioning of our bodies – we attribute feelings of well-being or pleasure to external factors and only become aware of our physiology when something is wrong. This tendency to address our physiology through human factors only when we are cold, hungry, tired or in pain ignores the possibilities of contributing to human health in broader, more positive ways.

Once machines became more 'intelligent' with electronics, the focus switched anyway from physiology to cognitive psychology, the study of how people's minds work, not just how their bodies function. And when intelligent machines starting connecting to each other to form intelligent systems, designers began to look towards sociology and anthropology for fresh answers. Whereas the age of Henry Dreyfuss – the industrial economy – dealt to a large extent in rational anthropometric calculation, a new age of design, focusing on the whole experience of user interaction, required altogether more subtle calibration.

The next stage of the progression, believes Moggridge, is in organizing all of today's intelligent systems within a sustainable whole that protects the environment. 'We're not there yet on that one,' says Moggridge, but it is clear that IDEO is right there in designing for the experience economy.

A new age of design, focusing on the whole experience of user interaction, required more subtle calibration

IDEO worked on the
landmark development
of the Airbus A3XX
aeroplane interior.
Concepts were created
for a simple, neutral
space which enhances
human comfort and avoids
the general sensation of
entering a machine.

The Amtrak Acela: the launch of the new North East Corridor express train service between Boston and Washington DC entailed the development of a totally new service strategy that is capable of competing effectively against the airlines. IDEO designed the total passenger experience of using this new service, from making the decision to travel to arrival and continuing beyond the rail destination.

By analyzing the total Amtrak passenger experience, IDEO identified ten steps in the 'journey': learning, planning, starting, entering, ticketing, waiting, boarding, riding, arriving and continuing. Each aspect was then addressed in relation to the next as part of the creation of a seamless experience.

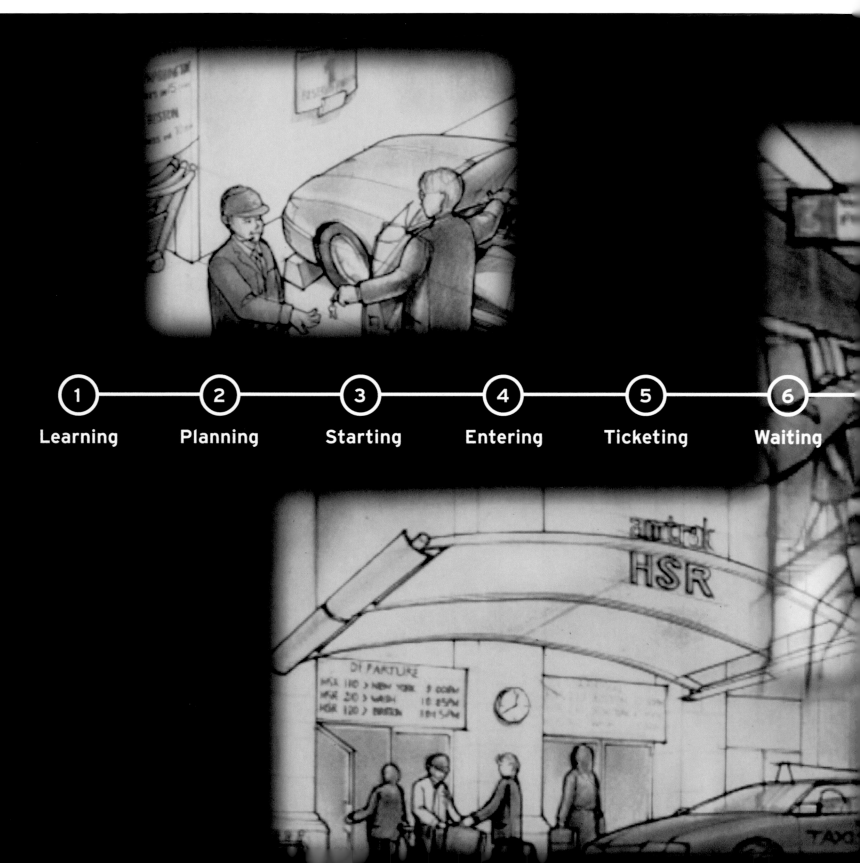

1 Learning   2 Planning   3 Starting   4 Entering   5 Ticketing   6 Waiting

7 Boarding

8 Riding

9 Arriving

10 Continuing

IDEO's design for Steelcase's Worklife showroom at Columbus Circle, New York, created a new model for the display of Steelcase furniture systems in order to feature product attributes and explore broader workplace issues. A number of product pods were strategically placed throughout the two selling floors. Within a condensed floor space new ways were developed to display furniture in the context of everyday use. Visitors now spend considerably longer in the showroom (up from around 40 minutes to nearly two hours per visit) and sales have increased by 25 per cent.

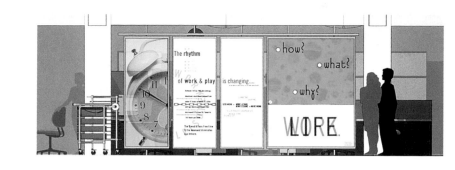

The Xerox Knowledge
Sharing Centre in
New York is Xerox's first
showroom accessible to
the public. Interactive
exhibits teach the unguided
visitor about the history
and future of documents
and about current Xerox
developments.

The Web Station for Streetspace. An internet-based service that offers users personalized information, e-mail and web browsing, this is an extremely rugged product for public spaces.

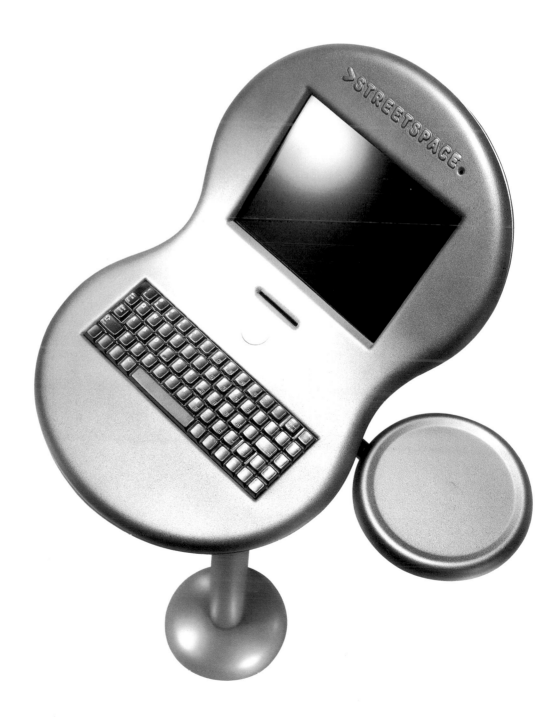

Thames Water Watercycle Pavilion, situated on the Millennium Dome site in Greenwich, London. An exhibition building to show the sophisticated technologies used in recycling the water that services the Dome. A glass building was constructed for the water treatment plant. The building is continuously covered in water from shower heads above. Inside, the watercycle system is explained in detail with engaging graphic information.

6 Speculative concepts

The best design feels as though it has been discovered... Discoveries just look right from the beginning, there is nothing arbitrary about them

Mike Nuttall, Co-Founder, IDEO

IDEO's future concepts for familiar everyday products range across many areas. Shown here are four of the ideas which emerged from a project to rethink the ubiquitous light switch.

One of the defining characteristics of IDEO is its passionate interest in designing speculative future concepts. Sometimes these advanced cultural research projects, positioned far ahead of market reality, are sponsored by commercial clients such as Steelcase, Epson or Kodak to explore some aspect of potential technology or user application. Often IDEO invests the time, resources and money itself to generate new thinking in areas as diverse as light switches, sandals, chocolate, intimate personal communicators or public transport for older people.

According to Tim Brown, former managing director of IDEO London, 'Our speculative projects position IDEO as an intelligent company keen to generate fresh ideas and share insights across all our offices and with our clients. If we don't create the space to conduct interesting experiments outside existing market and technological constraints, how else can we learn as an organization? And these projects are never just about making new things for its own sake. They are carefully chosen to give us the opportunity to explore new materials, for example, or new types of experiences, or ways to make technology beautiful.'

It is a philosophy that reflects IDEO leader David Kelley's insistence on a high level of intellectual curiosity within the firm's teams of designers and engineers in order to 'fake the future' with imagination and conviction. Curiosity is a hallmark of IDEO, says Robert Sutton of Stanford University: 'Designers at IDEO have a seemingly insatiable curiosity about the technology and process of product design. Indeed, they demonstrate a relentless curiosity about the factors of everyday life.' And, if directed in the right areas, curiosity inevitably leads to discovery. 'The best design feels as though it has been discovered,' says IDEO co-founder Mike Nuttall. 'It makes a forceful, compelling statement about how a thing should be. Discoveries just look right from the beginning. There is nothing arbitrary about them.'

Most organizations, whether service providers such as national broadcasters or global manufacturers such as appliance-makers, are intensely curious about the future. But few have exactly the right resources or knowhow to conduct a design forecasting experiment that combines pure speculation with informed prediction that cannot be easily dismissed. IDEO's skill is in achieving a balance between fantasy and practicality. Its proposals may sometimes stretch our credulity but never to the point at which the possibility can definitively be ruled out. This ability to challenge our capacity to change entrenched attitudes – whether dealing with the shape of a mobile phone or the use of a digital camera – has been much in demand during IDEO's first ten years. It is very much part of its culture, links directly to such client initiatives as the IDEO U concept, and builds substantially on expertise in visualizing and storyboarding user scenarios with fictional characters.

If we don't create the space to conduct experiments, how else can we learn?

When, for example, the British Broadcasting Corporation (BBC) wanted to explore the potential of Digital Audio Broadcasts (DAB), it turned for speculative digital radio product concepts to IDEO Europe. Among the nine ideas generated through brainstorming and scenario-building was a circular Family Radio that can memorize and save each family member's favourite programmes, and a Personal Radio that can learn about its busy user and automatically tune to the station most appropriate to his or her needs at different times of the day.

A third scenario looked at special-purpose radios used by one person in different situations: for 27-year-old Sheffield-based Viju the plumber, for example, a splash-proof Aqua Radio was designed with high sound quality, a recall facility to repeat the last five minutes of any broadcast and a stylish hook to hang the radio temporarily on a wall. There were also concepts for alarm, sports and 'my first' digital radios. The project's design expression in response to anticipated user behaviour brought the vision of digital radio broadcasting closer to home than any newspaper columnist's speculation or consultant's report had done previously.

When IDEO worked with a team of designers at Epson to look at the future of digital printing in the context of the rise in homeworking, there was also a focus on memory and experience, but with different outcomes. In exploring ways in which high-resolution digital printing of photographs, originally developed for offices, could fit into a domestic environment, the project generated a portfolio of intriguing, abstract objects. These included a wooden cabinet to house a 'drawer for drawings' and a design called 'mysterious thoughts' that covered the printer with a white fabric moving slightly as the print head travels back and forth. There were also proposals that delivered the print into a tray in an act reminiscent of darkroom developing, or supported it on a delicate wire frame. Each of these subtle concepts attempted to place the value on the printed image rather than the printer itself, reinventing work-based computer peripherals for the rituals of home life.

This spirit of reinvention is central to IDEO's speculative conceptual approach. When dealing with information appliances, there is no alternative but to fundamentally reappraise, believes Bill Moggridge. 'A camera is a good example of an information appliance,' he explains. 'Just a few years ago, a camera was a mechanical and optical instrument with a chemical film. Little by little the computer chips invaded. First it was automatic exposure, then auto-focus, and red-eye removal: now digital memory is replacing film. We still think of it as a camera though, dedicated simply to the task of capturing images, but it is not just a camera any more. It's a camera, an album and a way of editing and choosing. Somehow the design expression has to support all of these things.'

In a project with Kodak to explore the future of the digital camera, an IDEO team reappraised the fundamentals of how and why we take, store, share and manipulate images. Using Apple Micromedia technology, it convincingly 'faked the future' to show how a digital camera interface could work easily and intuitively. Many of the ideas generated by the study were later incorporated into the industrial design for Kodak's DC200 Digital Camera, an example of the market benefits that eventually come from hanging out on the wire of future possibilities.

IDEO designers have a seemingly insatiable curiosity

The light switch exploratory project was carried out in IDEO's San Francisco studio. The results, including those shown here, were exhibited at New York's Museum of Modern Art.

For Steelcase, operating as it does at the interface of architecture, furniture, user behaviour and new technologies, research of this kind is all-important. IDEO's speculative projects for the company have ranged from a home office furniture collection shown at the 100% Design show in London to the Q-concept, a futuristic battery-powered workstation controlled by a joystick on the armrest, which was developed to illustrate the need for new levels of adjustability in the work environment of the future.

A joint IDEO-Steelcase research study entitled Moving explored the future product and service needs of mobile workers, using imaginative office-based scenarios. Storylines ranged from the launch of a revolutionary hair-restoring cream on the technology campus of Chemcorp, an invented multinational, to the crisis 'incident room' set up in the corporate offices of the fictitious Vertigo Airlines following an air crash in Chile. These scenarios may not have been 'true to life', but the intricate character motivations and interactions were real enough to identify new product needs – and they were subsequently described in a video directed by Bill Moggridge and screened at Chicago's Neocon trade fair in 1996.

Bringing the future closer has implications not just for a company's technologies but also for its brands. An IDEO collection of future kitchen appliances with Matsushita, for example, showed ways in which the manufacturer's brand could portray the hybrid cultural values of east and west inherent to the Japanese breakfast. But for all the collaborative future-gazing with clients, the true character of IDEO's design curiosity is perhaps revealed by those speculative concepts it does entirely off its own bat.

The firm signalled its go-it-alone intentions early on when, in 1992, IDEO London took part in a 'product challenge' organized by the DesignAge action reseach programme at the Royal College of Art. The purpose of DesignAge was to show that in a world of an ageing population (50 per cent of Europe's adult population will be aged 50 or over by 2020) designers were capable of developing age-friendly design that included the needs and desires of older people. IDEO projected six years into the future to develop a series of user scenarios for an urban bus: in one of these, Agnes, a senior citizen, enjoys the warmth and safety of a draught-free bus shelter, and appreciates the way the bus docks with the shelter so there are no steps to climb; once aboard, she welcomes the comfort of a smooth ride, soft interior finishes and glare-free lighting. A far-fetched scenario given the harsh reality of London buses at the time? IDEO powerfully articulated a series of potential improvements, using existing technologies, some of which have since been implemented by London bus companies.

Design curiosity is revealed by projects IDEO does off its own bat

Since the early 1990s, IDEO's self-financed forays into the future have ranged from a sensual exploration of the rituals of eating chocolate to creative studies of tomorrow's flip-flop and light switches. It has looked at long-distance personal relationships, developing the Lovephone (with the hardware embedded in a suede pillow with red silk lips) and the Fuzzyphone (made of polar fleece for warm conversations on cold winter nights) in the USA. IDEO San Francisco also created the Kiss Communicator, a handheld device which enables lovers to blow each other electronic kisses across the world. This works by blowing into the central 'mouth' of the object — electronics translate the impulse into a series of pulsating lights which are then transmitted as a slow glow to your partner's equivalent device far away. If picked up and squeezed, your partner's device will repeat the message in complementary colours, so sealing an intimate bond of affection across distance. But if the device is left untouched, the glowing message will quickly fade.

In recent years, IDEO has become increasingly systematic in scanning the design horizon. In Europe, the firm joined a European Union-funded consortium called Maypole to develop speculative new interaction concepts for the extended family. Working alongside such organizations as Nokia Research, the Netherlands Design Institute and Helsinki University of Technology, an IDEO team studied two real-world communities — a school in Vienna and a scouting troop in Helsinki — before contributing to the design of conceptual products for informal communication as part of a two-year programme.

In the US, meanwhile, IDEO launched a six-month programme to evaluate trends in technology, Project 2010, and designed a series of future products for work, entertainment, medicine and sport, some of which were published in <u>Business Week</u>. Project 2010 demonstrated product innovations coming to a home or office near you soon: flexible liquid crystal displays that let you pull out a large screen from your cellphone; artificial intelligence that filters and prioritizes your e-mail; holography that generates moving 3D images in real time; and scanning technology that replaces credit cards with thumb prints. Walk into any IDEO studio while these speculative projects are going on and you could be forgiven for thinking the future has already arrived.

Self-financed forays into the future have ranged from studies of chocolate to light switches

This project for the BBC (British Broadcasting Corporation) by IDEO London set out to explore the potential of digital radio in a range of new concepts. Brainstorming generated design ideas that were built into user scenarios to explore the appearance and operation of the digital radios.

Displays on the radios show pictorial information to complement the audio programme, such as musician portraits, sports facts, programme guides or recording set-up information. Designs range from home radios that can be instantly personalized by family members to personal

portable radios and radios for the shower. Shown here: the Family Radio with speakers detatched (left) and attached (below right); and mother and child watch pictures whilst listening to a story (right).

110

User scenarios explore the operation of new digital radios in the IDEO London project for the BBC. Left: Viju the plumber tries out his waterproof 'shower radio'; right: Jean's Personal Digital Radio – a radio and web browser with a personal settings feature to suit her lifestyle.

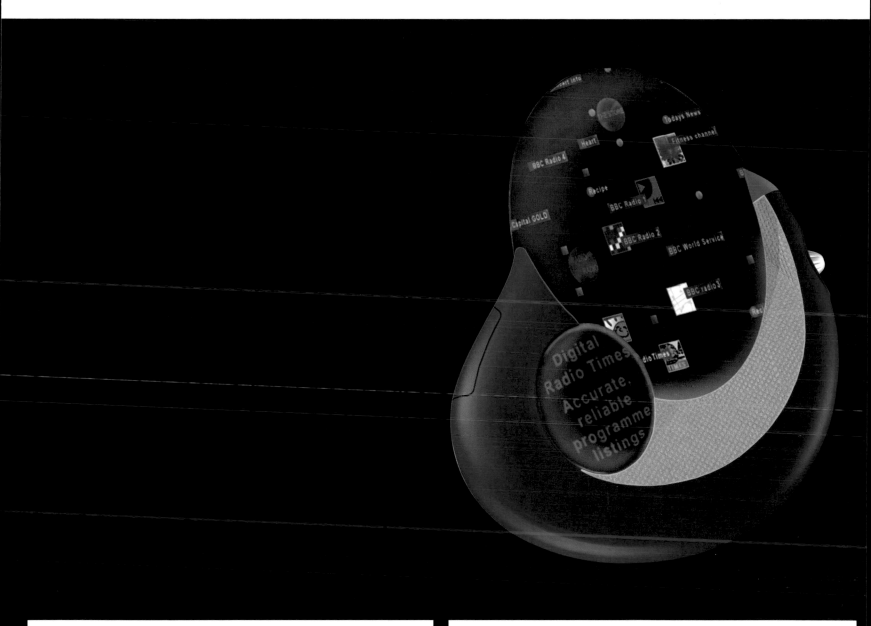

scenario description

Jean is woken by a telephone call; it's an emergency. She gets out of bed and starts to get ready. Jean switches on her personal Digital Radio in the bathroom to help her wake up. It automatically tunes into her usual channel for this time of the day.

She gets into her car and docks her personal Digital Radio to recharge the batteries. The radio communicates her car specific listening preferences, via Infra-Red (IR) link, to the in-car radio, so when she wants to listen to music the car radio suggests her favourite station. Her programme is interrupted by some travel news but luckily it will not affect her journey.

key ideas

• Specific stations for specific time - "MYradio".

• Agent driven learning system - watch me.

• **Car Docking** - powers battery.

• **Infra Red link** - personal radio can communicate preferences to other radios.

• Environment specific information - in the car she gets travel news.

scenario description

Jean arrives back home. As she moves from room to room her Digital Radio automatically links to the speakers in each room. She is listening to BBC Radio Music Plus as usual for this time in the morning.

Knowing she wants some music to go jogging to later, Jean records some music from the Fitness Channel. She stores it on a memory disc as she may want to use it again. The programme has already started but she is able to record it from the beginning.

After her run, Jean rests in the lounge and browses the latest copy of "Digital Radio Times". This magazine is downloaded once a week and gives Jean scheduling information as well as interesting articles. She sets her digital radio to view through her projector so she can see the text easily. As she views the schedule information, different programmes are subtly highlighted due to her preference and previous listening habits. She scans the information both visually and audibly.

key ideas

• **Speakers with infra-red connection** - auto, manual settings.

• Audio download to storage

• Recording from the start of programme

• Visual manipulation of information to show preference

• Audio Visual magazine

• Bulk download - probably at night.

• **Projected displays**

IDEO Japan and a team of designers at Epson collaborated to explore the future of digital printing in the context of a rise in homeworking. The result was a fresh and friendly approach to the design of machines that have now crossed the domestic threshold. Imperfect Perfection (below left) acknowledges with a bin that prints are often less than perfect. Mysterious Thoughts (right) presents the paper from under a table cloth like a note slipped under the door. Kinetic Deliverance (below right) has a paper tray that moves with the paper – only when the printer functions is the tray visible.

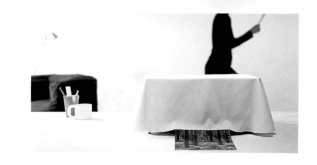

More concepts from
IDEO's project with Epson,
which looked at the future
of digital printing in the
home. Drawer for Drawings
(main image) presents
the printer as furniture.
Memory Developing (right)
uses a photo-kit analogy
for the printer.

Concept Q vacuum cleaner
for Hoover, designed for
an exhibition. All controls
are in the handle and the
dirt is collected in a
translucent canister.

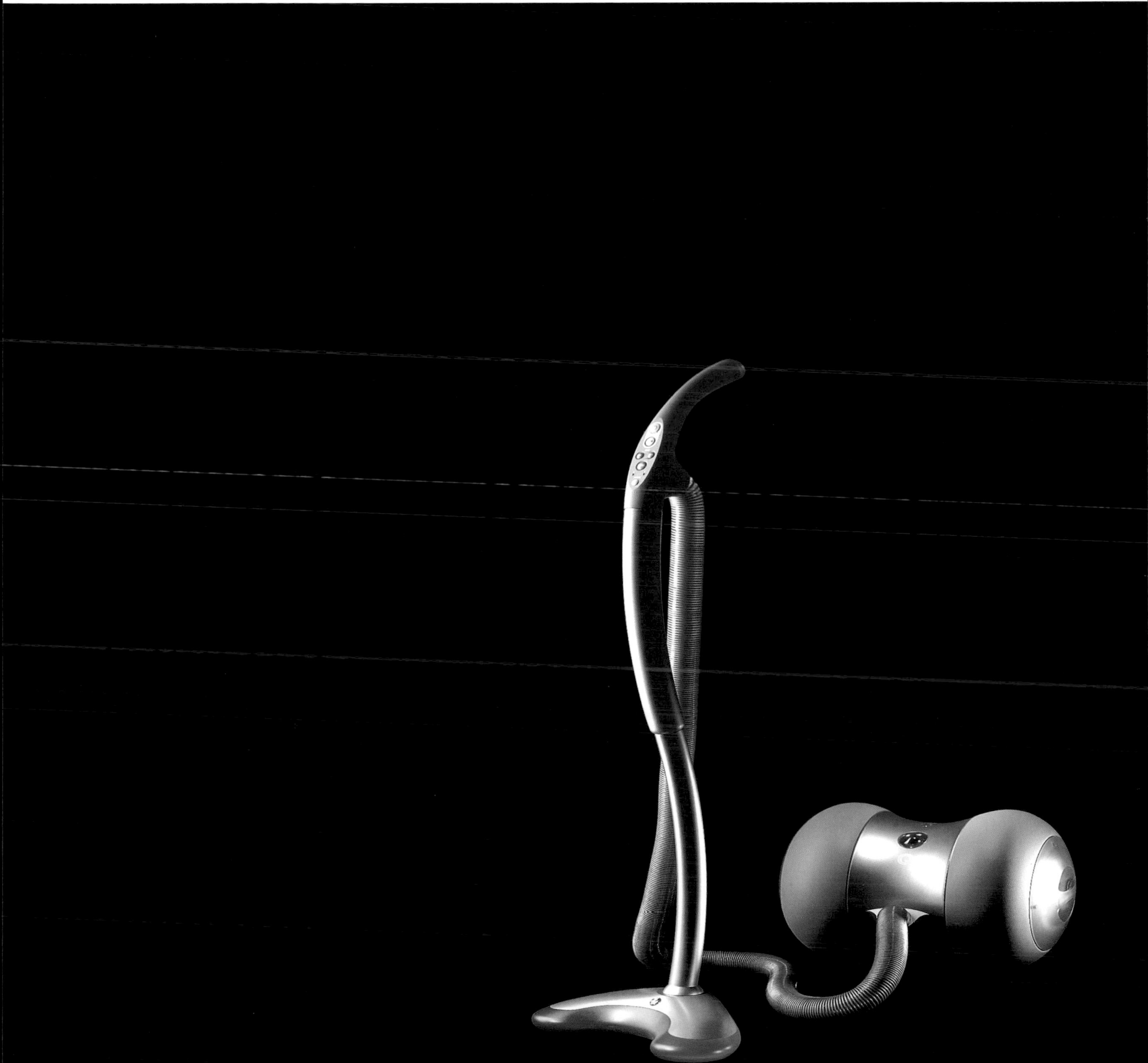

A conceptual exploration of chocolate. This project is an example of IDEO looking at a world of products rarely addressed by designers – in this case the emotional reaction to a favourite food. Shown here, left to right: a 'wishbone' chocolate that can be shared – leaving one person with the greater half; chocolate presented as a pill so you don't have to taste it if you don't like it; chocolate as the fruit of love – eat the chocolate before you reveal the filling; a chocolate that is eaten off the finger; a removable top provides a sneak preview of the filling to see if you like it; select your own filling and connect the nut and bolt; 'love me – love me not' chocolate; a strand at a time or throw it all into the mouth greedily; stir this chocolate into your after dinner coffee – the chocolate will melt and the liqueur seep into your coffee after which you eat the sweet; play with it, squeeze it and eat it when you're ready; and, finally, assemble the chocolate kit first by licking the edges, then enjoy.

118

A radio concept that explores the use of RDS (Radio Data System), commonly used in car radios. The screen gives information on programmes missed and opportunites to listen to them. It has preference settings for personal selections.

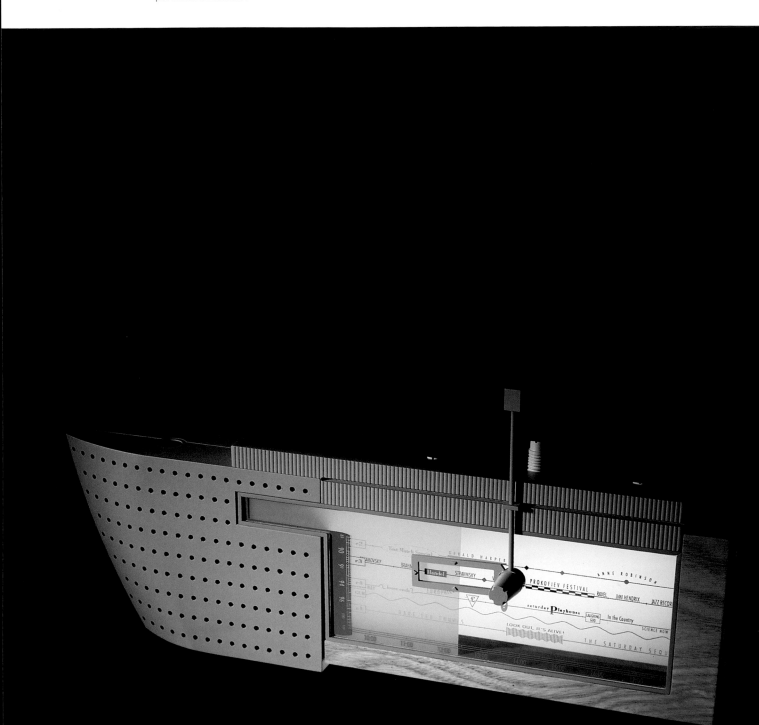

This conceptual project to explore the flip-flop was undertaken by the Palo Alto office. Each piece of footwear is a designer's personal interpretation of an iconic piece of West Coast culture.

120

The Kiss Communicator, developed by IDEO San Francisco, is a handheld device which allows lovers to blow each other kisses across distance. It works by blowing into the central 'mouth' of the object – electronics translate the impulse into a series of randomly lit LEDs, which are then transmitted as a slow glow to your partner's equivalent device far away. If picked up and squeezed, your partner's device will repeat the message in complementary colours. But if left untouched, the glowing message will fade quickly.

Home work furniture designed and made with Steelcase Strafor for the 100% Design exhibition, London, 1998. Products included an upholstered table, a wardrobe for filing and a trolley for the bed with connections for the computer. The collection of pieces demonstrated how functional task furniture could be given a suitable domestic aesthetic for use in a loft living space.

A'Toon is an interactive communication device for children. It is one of the concepts to emerge from the Maypole Project, a European Union-funded study of communication patterns in families and applications for new technologies. IDEO worked with a consortium of six European organizations to observe families, evaluate concepts and build and test prototypes.

N'Aut is an IDEO concept for a shell-like phone that you can see, feel, hear and customize to your own preference.

IDEO Japan worked on the conceptual development of a collection of future kitchen tools with Matsushita in order to respond to the hybrid cultural values of east and west inherent in the Japanese breakfast. The rice grinder/cooker (left) enables raw rice to be poured in at the top, ground and cooked to the desired consistency; the ground husk is kept in its own container for the making of pickles. A small two-slice toaster (centre) has an adjustable spring that allows breads of varying thicknesses to be toasted; the ceramic lid is also a toast rack. A water kettle (right) makes use of the heat dissipation from the top of the pot to warm either up to four teacups or the teapot.

In the Digimoda project, IDEO collaborated with the MIT Media Lab to address the human side of wearable computing. The work concentrated on two characters – a woman called Kio and a man called Guy – to explore the personal significance of wearable computing and to try to understand how a single-core technology could be utilized and interpreted in many different ways.

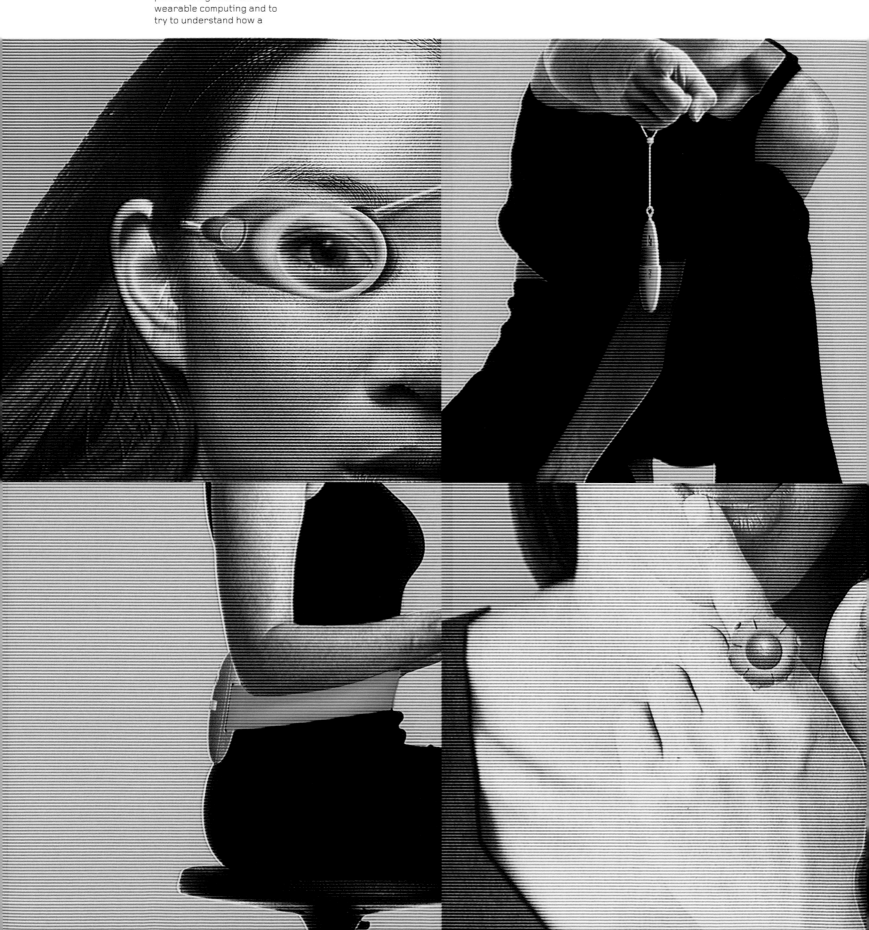

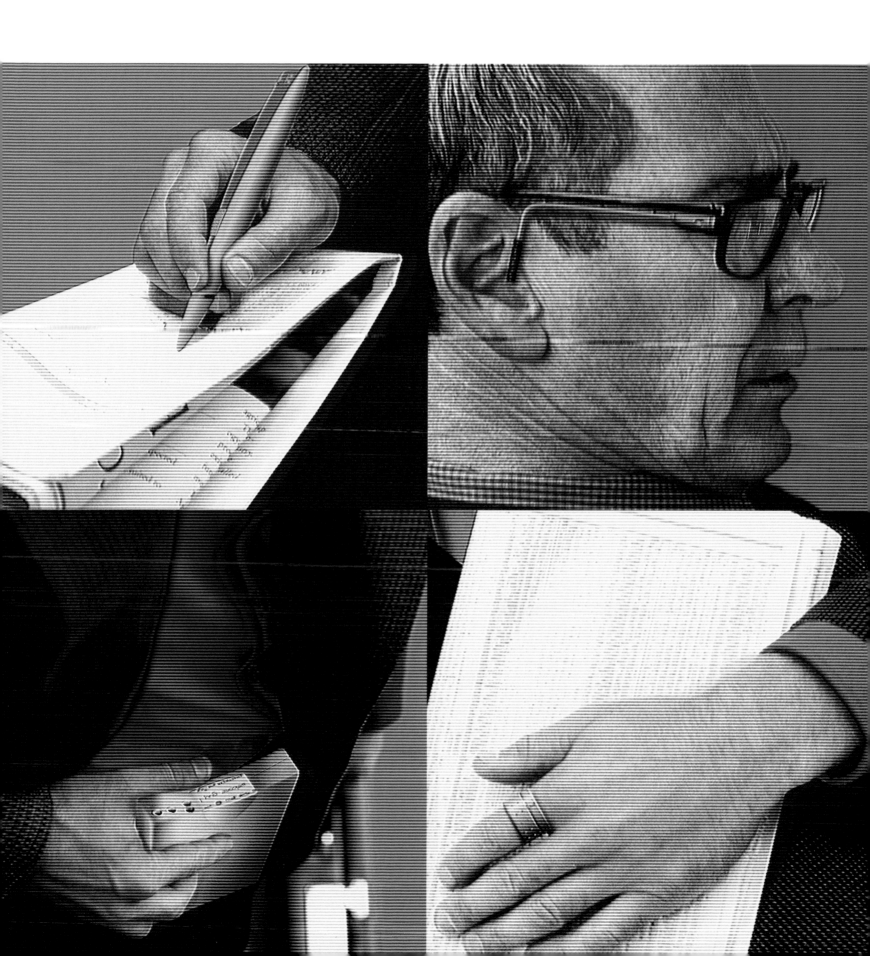

The Q Concept for Steelcase was developed to illustrate the need for new levels of adjustability in the work environments of the future. Q moves on its own battery power, controlled by a joystick on the armrest. The user recalls personal preferences by inserting a personal digital assistant into a slot, sits in the workchair and drives to be near to the team members who are sharing the work at hand. The ideas expressed in this prototype build on an extensive body of research into changing workplace practices, including user observations and video ethnography.

The Transmeta Webslate:
a concept for a handheld
information appliance which
uses a pen to interact with
the internet. It is enabled
by a new micro processor,
the Crusoe. Modules can be
added, for example a camera
for videoconferencing,
GPS for navigation, audio
speakers and controls for
downloading music.

Without Thought was the title of a workshop held in Japan in September 1999, its aim to create 'designs for unconsciousness'. In-house designers, brought together from different companies by the Diamond Design Management Network, collaborated with IDEO in Tokyo to create concepts that touch the senses and trigger memories shared by people. Ideas such as the CD Player (left) and Sponge Scale (right) were developed and visualized for an exhibition.

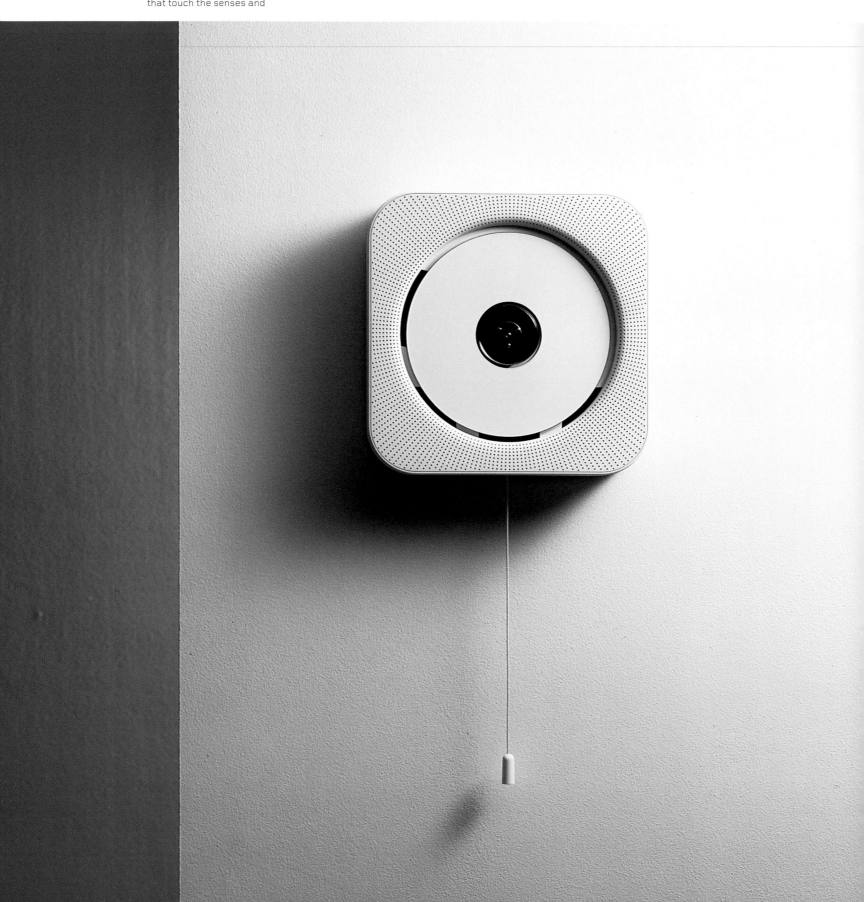

More concepts from the
Without Thought workshop,
Japan, 1999, which sought
to examine the idea of
unconscious design:
(below) Computer Paper
Display; (right) Clock.

At the turn of the millennium IDEO spent six months evaluating trends in technology and lifestyle to create a set of concept predictions for the year 2010. New products for work, entertainment, medicine and sports were designed. Project 2010 was published in <u>Business Week</u>, 6 March 2000. Some of the work is shown in the following pages. My Agent (below) is a PDA (personal digital assistant) of the future, which looks after money, keys, credit cards, beepers and TV remotes. The E-quill (right) captures messages and beams them to the agent PDA.

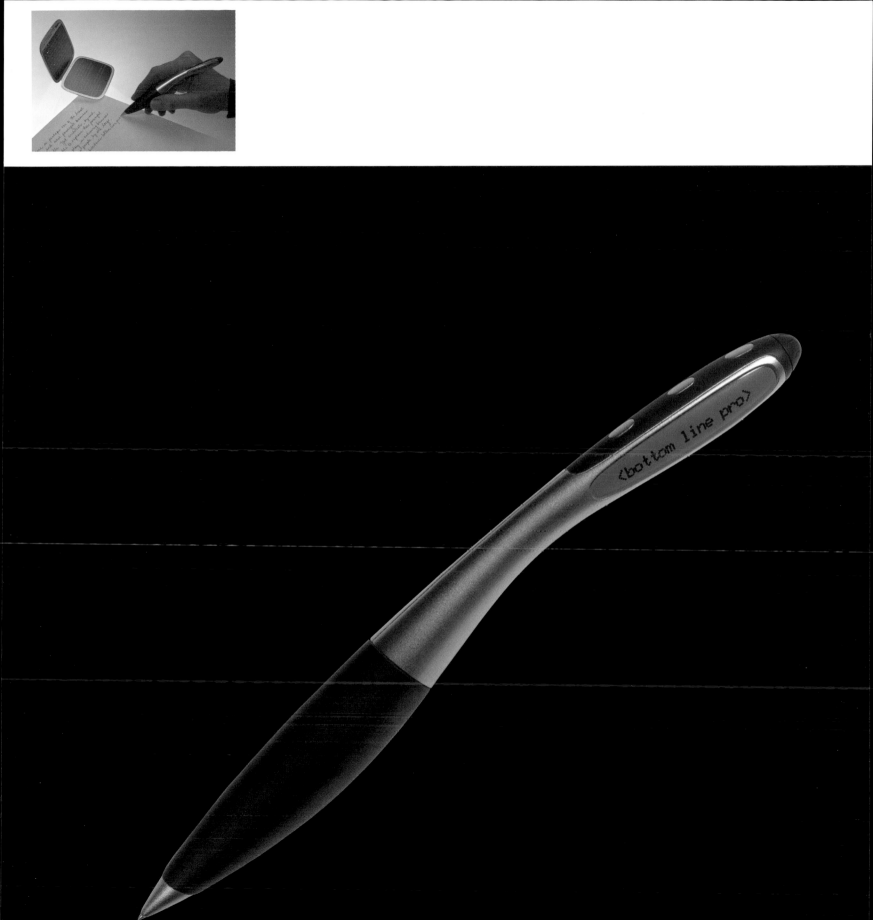

One of Project 2010's most convincing concepts, the Tube is tomorrow's laptop. A flexible LCD (liquid crystal display) provides a large pull-out screen to read web-based information. Dials on the Tube (right) show messages or data received. Low voltage lets a pared-down processor do most tasks; wireless access connects the user to the internet for such heavy-duty applications as language translation.

More views of the Tube, from Project 2010. Voice recognition makes a keyboard optional as flexible liquid crystal displays change the form of tomorrow's laptop from a square to a scroll that rolls out. Reading web-based information on the Tube's LCD screens (right) can be akin to reading a newspaper, as two pages emerge from the product's central spine.

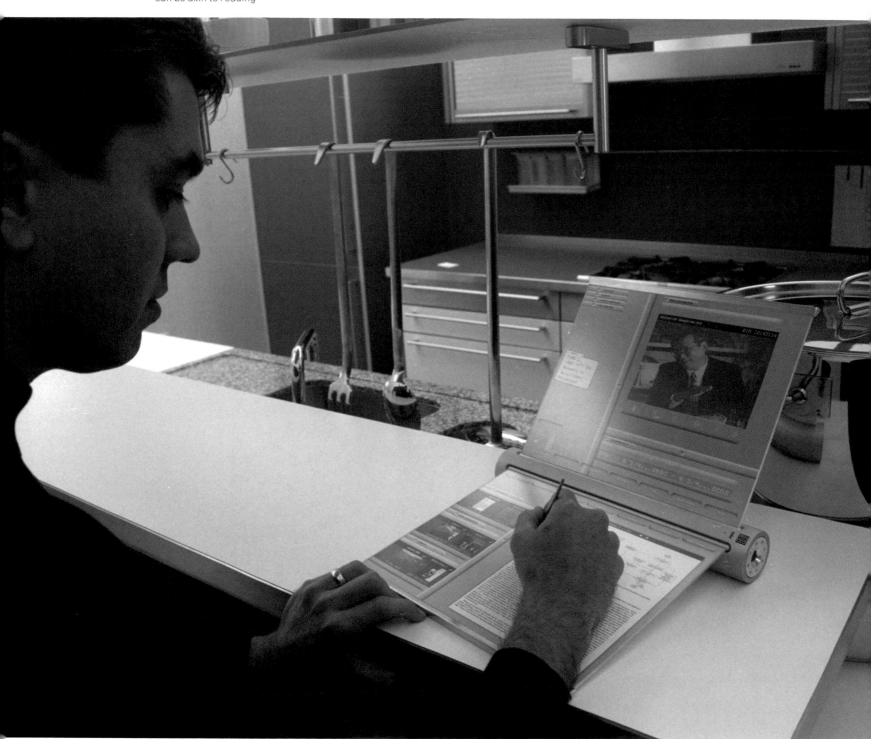

From the Project 2010 portfolio, the Sports Watch does everything without being bulky thanks to low power, small sensors and sticky gel-adhesive backing. It times your exercise, monitors vital statistics and analyzes performance. The hydro-gel is matched to human skin, so that as your skin stretches, the gel stretches along with it. Photovoltaic cells provide the power. Performance data is uploaded to your PDA (personal digital assistant) for analysis.

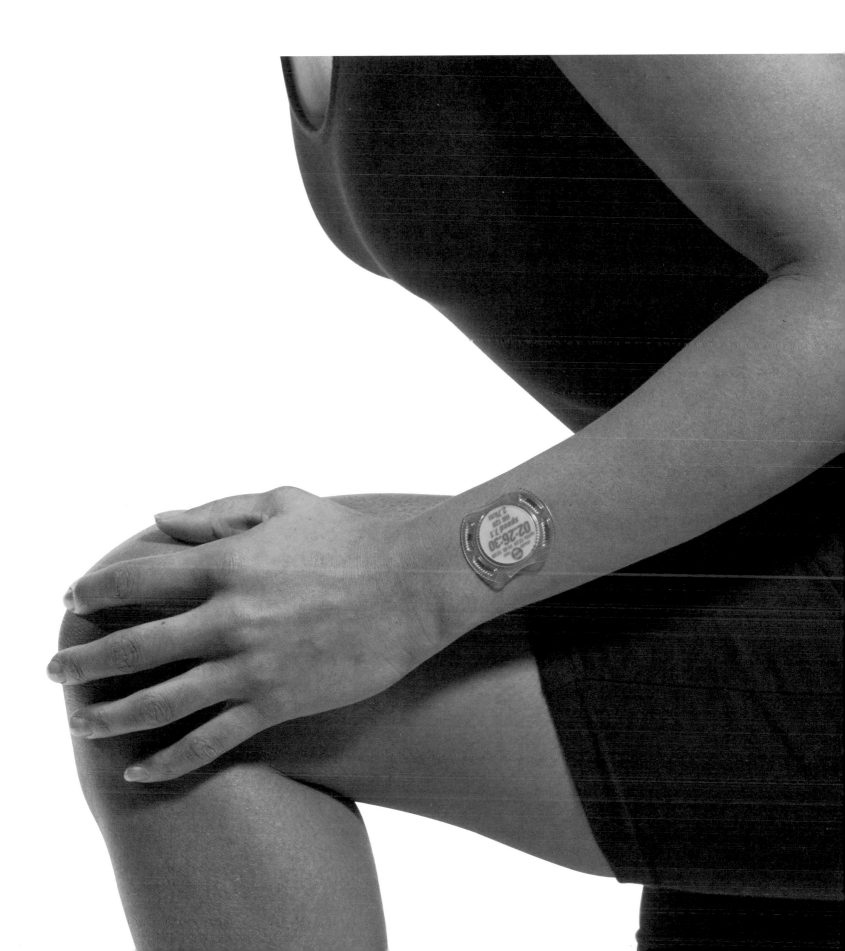

A low-powered phone, which is lightweight, ear-mounted and equipped with one follow-you number. It also connects to the internet.

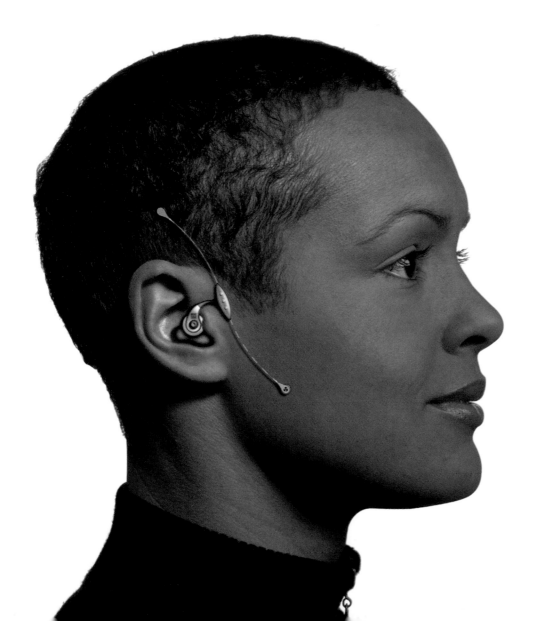

Technojewellery. GPS-embedded toe jewellery signals 'turn left' towards your destination. Linked to satellites via the PDA power plant at your belt or in your bag, GPS Toes explore a new part of the body for wearable technology.

Cellphone Rings (below): This cellphone is a jewel. Earpiece and mouthpiece telephony are intuitively embedded in finger jewellery. When not in use, the rings are flipped around on the thumb and little finger for comfort and adornment.

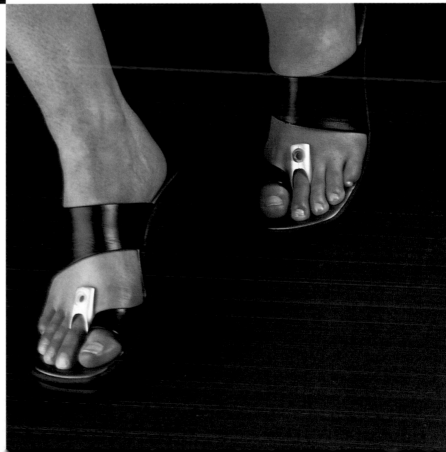

IDEO is a new animal and we're still learning how to exercise it. None of us really understands all the nuances

Tim Brown, Chief Executive Officer, IDEO

Tim Brown, new CEO of IDEO, is committed to continuing the firm's radical development of new models of design practice.

In January 2001, on the eve of its tenth anniversary, there were changes at the top of IDEO. Founder David Kelley relinquished the hands-on role of chief executive officer to concentrate on forging new strategic alliances externally, as chairman of the firm. Englishman Tim Brown, a former director of the London and San Francisco offices, was appointed to replace him as CEO and president, based in Palo Alto. For Tim Brown, the step-up marked a logical progression for an industrial designer who played a prominent role in forging IDEO's innovation culture during its first decade in business. Immediately, Brown declared his intention to remain true to the radical instincts that propelled IDEO to international attention under Kelley's stewardship.

'In founding IDEO, David Kelley changed the rules of the product design firm in terms of how you practise, the scale at which you practise, and the calibre of clients you can attract,' explains Brown. 'Up until then, US design firms were still modelled on the lines of Henry Dreyfuss and Raymond Loewy – they were small, craft-based operations, working with a handful of great clients in the recognizable discipline of industrial design. But IDEO has gone down a new road, bringing disciplines together in new ways, creating entirely new disciplines, reinventing the whole notion of what industrial design is all about. As far as I'm concerned, that process will continue and accelerate over the next few years.'

Brown sees IDEO's future culture as having three distinct interlocking strands: consulting, learning and entrepreneurial. The consulting strand, he believes, belongs to a European tradition brought to Silicon Valley by Bill Moggridge and Mike Nuttall and to which IDEO has added new layers of user-oriented sophistication and technical depth. The learning strand has been enhanced through IDEO's close links with Stanford University, its human factors research, its emphasis on teaching corporations how to innovate and its belief in the value of advanced speculative concepts. The entrepreneurial strand is where IDEO is set to drive change most powerfully – already there have been initiatives in the areas of business strategy, licensing and venture funding.

According to Mike Nuttall, 'The traditional design practice model of clients paying for time plus materials has been quite robust, but now it is dated. The design profession needs to move towards new business models. Designers need to share more of the risk and more of the profits and success with their clients. Earning royalties, taking equity in start-ups and developing our own products are all models of the future we're working on.'

High up on this new business agenda is a desire, in Tim Brown's words, 'to build a culture of strategy to match our culture of innovation'. In the past, says Brown, IDEO often made a wonderful job of designing the wrong product because the business strategy it was given to work with was wrong. 'If we want to mature as a design firm and be smarter, the next step is to go upstream to understand the client's business intent,' declares David Kelley.

But developing an IDEO offer to design the strategy prior to designing the product hasn't been easy. In the late 1990s the firm invested in a British design strategy start-up, The Fourth Room, but progress was a struggle and IDEO sold its interest within a couple of years. 'Clearly we don't want to compete directly with the McKinseys of this world,' says Brown, 'but there is still a role for us to play in helping clients work out what they want to do at the outset. It may be that we form an alliance with an established player in this area, or build strategy expertise organically within IDEO in the same way we have done with human factors consulting. Already we have Harvard MBAs coming to work at IDEO.'

One example of IDEO's determination to break out of the old business model of design practice was its acquisition of Palo Alto toy development and licensing company Skyline. It now designs and develops toys for a range of major US manufacturers, including Hasbro and Mattel, on a royalty basis. The firm also set up IDEO Ventures, a corporate venturing fund which has already invested in several companies via the mechanism of providing design services in return for equity.

IDEO has gone down a new road, reinventing industrial design practice

Two examples of toys designed by Skyline, the toy development and licensing company in Palo Alto, now acquired by IDEO. Left: the FingerBlaster, a hugely successful toy that shoots over 100 feet; right: the Aerobie – a football that spirals and spins.

If the idea of a group of designers and engineers becoming venture capitalists really pushes the envelope, it also makes good business sense for a firm working in an area such as Silicon Valley, where the lure of high-tech start-ups can drain you of your best people. An investment in Handspring, a Silicon Valley company established by the founders of the Palm Pilot, has even taken IDEO into manufacturing. A new product, an eyemodule, has been produced under IDEO's own brand, Blocks Products.

Of course, investing in start-ups, manufacturing your own products, negotiating licensing deals and waiting for royalties to accrue are activities that entail a much higher degree of risk than just charging out your studio time. 'We'll need to spread our bets,' says Tim Brown, but he is determined that IDEO should grasp the initiative as design practice generally seeks to break out into new areas. 'Industrial design has gone through a constant process of reinvention,' he explains, pointing to new landmarks achieved by Loewy and his contemporaries on the East Coast in the 1940s, by British and German consultants in the 1960s, and by the main Silicon Valley players in the 1980s and 1990s. 'In a digital age, industrial design has become a dead discipline. The material of industrial design today is as much about the virtual as it is about the physical – as much about behaviours and experiences as about mechanical objects.'

It is IDEO's capacity for change, its suppleness as an organization, which unites external observers in the view that it will be in the vanguard of whatever new directions evolve in design practice. 'The design profession has changed dramatically in the 60 years of its existence,' according to Barry Katz, Professor of Design at the California College of Arts and Crafts in San Francisco. 'The individualist has given way to the multi-disciplinary team, the styling of surfaces has evolved into a concern with the totality of the product, short-term economic considerations have been supplemented with an ecological, educational and ethical perspective. The most significant aspect of the transformation of design, however, has been the growing recognition of the partnership of designer, client and end user in the success of a product. This continuum is where the greatest strides have been made and where the greatest challenges are still to be found. IDEO's capacity for artistic, technical and cultural research positions it ideally to explore these opportunities.'

By forming around a fusion of the design and engineering disciplines, by developing an innovation process driven by the twin engines of creative brainstorming and rapid prototyping, by consolidating expertise in technology and manufacturing, by designing user interactions and experiences, by investing in advanced future concepts, and by exploring business strategy and venture funding – by doing all of these things, IDEO has consistently remodelled notions of practice. Down its 'street' of studios, labs and workshops in Palo Alto, and across its international network of differently shaped and flavoured offices, that restless dynamism shows no sign of abating. As David Kelley suggests, 'The big challenge is working out how to do things that design companies have never done before, nor even thought about doing.'

The big challenge is to do things that design companies have never done before

The NCR Knowledge Lab in London wanted to present an engaging but controlled method of giving lobby visitors a sense of the work going on inside the organization. This playful installation uses real goldfish in an aquarium to control the display of a database containing the Lab's research areas, projects and personnel. A video camera and a sophisticated computer program track the random movements of the fish, using the changing positions to map graphics on a large plasma display above the tank. The result is informative and compelling, helping to reinforce opinions about the Knowledge Lab's work as a creative and humanistic contribution to NCR as much as a technological one.

The Handspring Visor and eyemodule is a new product from the founders of the Palm Pilot. It is an expandable computer with an expansion slot that accepts a variety of Springboard modules, providing paging, GPS devices, games and more. The eyemodule was designed specifically for the Handspring's innovative Springboard expansion slot by IDEO and manufactured by Blocks Products, an IDEO company. The project's focus on manufacturing reflects IDEO's own expansion as a product design firm into new development areas.

Scout Electromedia's Modo is a wireless handheld device that delivers up-to-date information on practically everything to do, see and eat in the city. Targeting young, active adults in places like San Francisco, New York and Los Angeles, Modo provides its users with instant access to movies, music, museums and more, while providing its advertisers with a desirable demographic market group.

Biometrics Bloid installation
in the new Wellcome Wing
of the Science Museum,
London. IDEO developed
the interaction design and
prototyping of this morphing
installation, which allows
you to visualize what rapid
ageing or gender change
might look like.

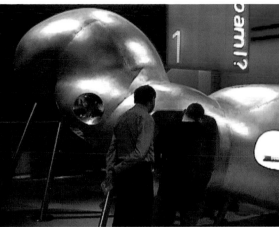

Stanford University Learning Lab is a global research institution dedicated to developing new learning methods, tools and spaces. The Learning Lab felt that traditional approaches to space planning would not successfully capture its culture and ideas. IDEO looked broadly at the physical, social and cultural aspects of life on campus for students, Lab staff and university faculty. It became clear that the building itself could not satisfy the needs of the Lab, but a holistic approach was needed considering technology, protocols and processes. The screen wall shown here is a landmark for the Learning Lab, communicating the Lab's purpose, providing shelter for a range of activities from informal gatherings to larger groups, and giving easy access to technology.

Electrotextiles Phone:
a first-generation
mobile phone which uses
electrotextile technology
to allow it to become
flexible. For the first time,
the surface of the product
is as intelligent as the
components inside.

'SpyFishing' has been jointly developed by H2Eye and IDEO. It reinvents the marine researcher's ROV (remote-operated vehicle) as a leisure experience. The SpyFish is a miniature remote-controlled submarine equipped with video cameras, connected via a slender cable to a display screen at the surface. The user watches real-time video with additional overlayed information and interacts with the SpyFish via a wireless hand control. Technical innovation by H2Eye has resulted in an advanced ROV – safe, compact and modular. An interdisciplinary design team has defined 'SpyFishing' as an iconic, intuitive and immersive experience.

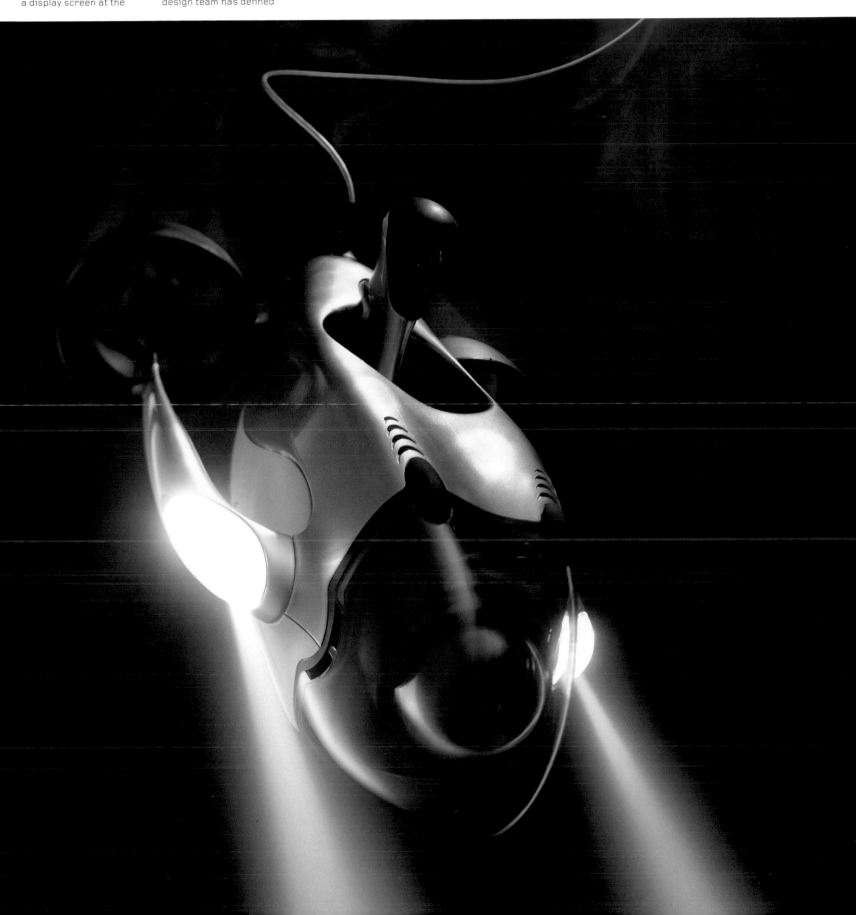

158 Acknowledgements

Many thanks to all these creative people at IDEO and elsewhere, and apologies to anyone inadvertently omitted

Matt Adams	Stacey Chang	Dick Grant	Anne Linden
Gretchen Addi	Larry Cheng	Jeff Grant	Aaron Lipner
Dirk Ahlgrim	Ben Chow	Phil Grebe	Dave Littleton
Athena Anagnostopoulous	Johnson Chow	Neil Grimmer	Tanisha Lloyd
Carl Anderson	Michael Chung	Clive Grinyer	Chris Loew
Sue Anderson	Scott Clark	Alex Grishaver	David Lyons
Dominick d'Andrea	Janet Collin	Alexander Grunsteidl	Ian MacColl
Heather Andrus	Jim Collins	Jon Guerra	Peter Macdonald
Bob Arko	Monika Conway	Hans Haenlein	Bruce MacGregor
Charles Ash	Sean Corcorran	Patrick Hall	Nick Maddix
Steve Atkins	Peter Coughlan	Amy Han	Dave Mallard
Nelson Au	Chris Cowart	Scott Hand	Conor Mangat
Chris Avis	Deuce Cruse	Jeremiah Harmsen	Wendy March
Jochen Backs	Tracy Currer	Gerry Harris	Matt Marsh
Ted Barber	Martin Darbyshire	Mark Harrison	Heather Martin
Gretchen Barnes	Jorge Davies	Robert Hartmann	Neil Martin
John Bauer	Phil Davies	Greg Hayes	Ippei Matsumoto
Oliver Bayley	Jennifer Davis	Sam Hecht	Bob McCaffrey
Richard Bayliss	Douglas Dayton	Joseph Hei	Nacho Mendez
Ela Ben-Ur	Andy Deakin	Matthew Hern	Michael Meyer
Stacy Benjamin	Bud DeLisle	Steve Heron	Mike Mills
Steve Berry	Dan DeRuntz	Graham Hicks	Alex Mitchell
Mark Biasotti	Otto DeRuntz	Lloyd Hicks	David Moal
Max Bielenberg	Markus Diebel	Yas Hirai	Sigi Moeslinger
Tim Billing	Monina Dolan	Dave Hixson	Bill Moggridge
Alison Black	Erich Domingo	Phil Hobson	Hal Monson
Dave Blakeley	Nick Dormon	Andy Hodge	Howard Montgomery
Nicole Bloom	Gregg Draudt	Ed Holman	Sarah Morris
Elaine Boiko	Dave Duncanson	Kathleen Holman	Tim Moulton
Martin Bone	Fred Dust	Jonah Houston	Raj Narayanan
Martin Bontoft	Lisa Dutra	Kuoyong Huang	Kevin Nason
Doug Bourn	Peter Ehling	Alison Humphries	Trae Neist
Sarah Boyd	Tom Eich	Mat Hunter	Mark Nichols
Dennis Boyle	Kristiana Elite	Dickon Isaacs	Dana Nicholson
Brendan Boyle	Thomas Enders	Takeshi Ishiguro	Greg Niejadlik
Paul Bradley	Trygve Faste	Mark Jones	Mike Nuttall
Duane Bray	Jim Feuhrer	Jared Judson	Nick Oakley
John Brassil	Mark Fisher	Cliff Jue	Steve O'Connor
Jacob Brauer	Jeanne Fitzgerald	Jon Kaplan	John O'Fallon
Phil Braunberger	Chris Flink	David Kelley	Jerry O'Leary
Scott Brenneman	Jesse Fourt	Tom Kelley	Jake Olefsky
Tim Brooke	Chris Frank	Duncan Kerr	Wendy Ong
Tim Brown	Roberto Fraquelli	Daniel Kim	Aura Oslapas
Juan Bruce	Cheri Fraser	Ed Kirk	Dan Ostrower
Mark Buchalter	Alycia Freeman	Scott Klinker	Thomas Overthun
Marion Buchenau	Frank Friedman	Ron Klutts	Annetta Papadopoulos
Colin Burns	Naoto Fukasawa	Leo Kopelow	Lynda Patrick
Andrew Burroughs	Jane Fulton Suri	Chris Kurjan	Tony Patron
Alison Camplin	Derek Fung	John Lai	Jennifer Pattee
Sarah Campbell	Nacho Germade	John Lake	Ed Pearce
Kristine Chan	Theo Gillman	Martin Langkau	Ali Pearlman
Lizardo	David Gilmore	David Law	Todd Pelman
Mark Chance	Roshi Givechi	Craig Lawrence	Roger Penn
Ana Chang	Joost Godee	Simon Leach	Alex Pereira
Kuen Chang	Marcus Gosling	Stephanie Lee	David Peschel
	Joe Graceffa	Rick Lewis	

Henry Philips
Anthony Piazza
Ed Porto
Tim Prachar
Dave Privitera
Ilya Prokopoff
Tim Proulx
Graham Pullin
Reynaldo Quintana
Harald Quintus-Bosz
John Raff
Tony Rastatter
Aldis Rauda
David Reinfurt
David Rinaldis
Erick Rios
Jason Robinson
Mark Roomor
Owen Rogers
Matt Rohrbach
Tony Ross
Tony Rossetti
Gordon Row
Benjamin Rush
Alexey Salamini
Gitta Salomon
Frances Samalionis
Craig Sampson
Rudy Samuels
Eric Saperstein
Robin Sarre
Gerd Schmieta
Jan Schmieta
Todd Schulte
Gary Schultz
Dan Schwartz
Amy Schwartz
Leon Segal
Steve Senatore
Rudy Servande
Aaron Sevier
Jan Seyberth
Maura Shea
Larry Shubert
George Simons
Pete Simpson
Adam Skaates
Peter Skillman
Aaron Sklar
Andrzej Skoskiewicz
John Smith
Alan South
Paul South
Ken Staal
Lars Stalling
Thomas Stegmann

Bill Stewart
Danny Stillion
Phil Stob
John Stoddard
Suzy Stone
Mike Strasser
Chris Stringer
Scott Stropkay
Ian Sumner
Rickson Sun
Vae Sun
Andy Switky
Craig Syverson
Steve Takayama
Elisha Tal
Joe Tan
Marc Tanner
Jim Tappol
Ben Tarbell
Brad Taylor
Ricca Tezuchi
Martin Thaler
Chase Thompson
Cale Thompson
Wink Thorne
Iain Thorpe
David Tonge
Drew Trainor
Rebecca Trump
Sam Truslow
Grace Tseng
Greg Tuzin
Greg Twiss
Axel Unger
Anne Van der Linden
Steve Vassallo
Velma Velazquez
Bernard Veronesi
Kevin Von Essen
Stephen Wahl
Pontus Wahlgren
Bryan Walker
Erik Wang
Joe Watson
David Webster
Christopher
Weeldreyer
Katrin Wegener
Denis Weil
Jeff Weintraub
David Weissburg
Donna Westwood
Bryan White
Symon Whitehorn
Scott Whitman
Dan Wilkins

Alison Willard
Scott Wilson
Clint Woesner
Melsa Wong
Tim Wood
Bill Wurz
Gretchen Wustrack
Joseph Yang
Andre Yousefi
Jim Yurchenco
Mark Zeh
Rico Zorkendorfer
Robert Zuchowski
Sal Zuno

Amtrak
093 Amtrak Acela

Durrell Bishop
118 IDEO RDS Radio Concept

Roberto Carra
032 Palo Alto office interior
036–041 Palo Alto office interiors

Richard Davies
092 Airbus: A3XX Aeroplane
Interior Concept
100–101 Thames Water: Watercycle Pavilion

A. Dovifat
082 Steelcase Strafor: 1+1 Furniture system

Rick English
011 Samsung; TotalMedia
016 Samsung: SimpleMedia
027 Microsoft: Mouse
043 IDEO Tech Box
049 Quadlux: Flashbake oven
054–055 Berkley: Fishing reels
058 Cisco: IP Phone
067 Nike: V8 Eyewear
071 NEC: M500 Monitor
075 Polaroid: I-Zone
078 3Com: Connect Cable Modem

Don Fogg
024 GRiD Inc. Compass Computer

Beverley Harper
065 Logitech: Wingman Formula Force
104–107 IDEO Light switches
116–117 IDEO Chocolates
120–121 IDEO Kiss Communicator

Sasaki Hidetoyo
072 NEC: LT84 LCD Projector
084–085 INAX: The Tile Project
112–114 Epson: Printables
126–127 Matsushita: Japanese Breakfast
132–135 Diamond Design Management
Network: Without Thought

IDEO
011 IBM: CPU
026 Apple: Mouse
034–035 Essen Exhibition,1996
094–095 Amtrak 10 points of journey
109–111 BBC: Digital Radio Concepts
124 IDEO: A'Toon Maypole Project
125 IDEO: N'aut Telephone Concept

128–129 IDEO/MIT Digimoda Concepts
150 NCR Installation
153 Science Museum: Biometrics Bloid
154–155 Stanford University:
Stanford Learning Lab
156 Electrotextiles: Soft Phone

David Joseph
098 Xerox: Xerox Knowledge
Sharing Centre

Youngsil Jung
050 LG Electronics: Dishwasher
066 LG Electronics: Washing machine

Martin Langfield
108 BBC: Digital Radio Concept

Nick Marrick & Hedric Blessing
080 Steelcase: Pathways Furniture System

Pete McArthur
083 Vecta: Kart Chair

John McCallum
064 Acco: Stapler

Milliot+ Edwards
017 Samsung: SyncMaster 400
and 500 TFT Monitors

Steven Moeder
010 Dell: Optiplex
008+012 IDEO Shopping Trolley
013 Pepsi: Twist 'n Go
014 Oral-B: Toothbrushes
050 Brivo Box, Whirlpool Oven
052 Audible Inc.: MobilePlayer
053 3Com: Palm V
056 Bridge Medical: Sentry
057 Eli Lilly: Humulin/Humalog Insulin Pen
062 3Com: Ergo Audrey
063 SoftBook Press: SoftBook Reader
068 Logitech: CyberMan 2
069 Merloni: The Home Smart Monitor
070 NEC: Multimedia Monitor
073 NetSchools Inc.: Netschool Computer
076 PRS: Photochemical Recycling System
081 Details: Stella Keyboard
099 Streetspace: The Web Station
115 Hoover: Concept Q Vacuum Cleaner
119 IDEO Flip-Flop exploration
130 Steelcase: Q Concept
131 Transmeta: Webslate
136–144 IDEO 2010 Concepts
145 IDEO Technojewellery

149 Skyline toys
151 Handspring Inc: Visor;
and Blocks Products: eyemodule
152 Scout Electromedia: Modo

Jeff Nelson
060–061 GM/Hughes: Electric Car
Charging project

Ian O'Leary
059 Ford: MidLine In-Car Audio System

Psion Infomedia
077 Psion Infomedia: Wavefinder

Francois Robert
015 Midwest Dental: AirTouch
Air Abrasive System

Sharon Risecorph
033+042 San Francisco office interior

John Ross
122–123 IDEO: Furniture Concepts
for 100% Design

Steelcase
096–097 Steelcase: NY Worklife

Jason Tozer
157 H2Eye: Spyfish

Mark Tuschman
020+021 Mike Nuttall, Bill Moggridge,
David Kelley
148 Tim Brown

Joe Watson
044–045 Sand Hill Challenge

Tom Wedell
048 Steelcase: Leap Chair
074 Polaroid: PopShots
079 Steelcase: Leap Chair

Mel Yates
031 IDEO London group picture

THE DAYS ARE JUST PACKED

Other Books by Bill Watterson
___

Calvin and Hobbes

Something Under the Bed Is Drooling

Yukon Ho!

Weirdos from Another Planet

The Revenge of the Baby-Sat

Scientific Progress Goes "Boink"

Attack of the Deranged Mutant Killer Monster Snow Goons

Treasury Collections
___

The Essential Calvin and Hobbes

The Calvin and Hobbes Lazy Sunday Book

The Authoritative Calvin and Hobbes

The Indispensable Calvin and Hobbes

THE DAYS ARE JUST PACKED

A Calvin and Hobbes Collection by Bill Watterson

SCHOLASTIC INC.
New York Toronto London Auckland Sydney

Calvin and Hobbes is distributed internationally by Universal Press Syndicate.

No part of this publication may be reproduced in whole or in part, or stored in a retrieval system, or transmitted in any form or by any means, electronic, mechanical, photocopying, recording, or otherwise, without written permission of the publisher. For information regarding permission, write to Andrews and McMeel, a Universal Press Syndicate Company, 4900 Main Street, Kansas City, MO 64112.

ISBN 0-590-47988-1

The Days Are Just Packed copyright © 1993 by Bill Watterson. All rights reserved. Published by Scholastic Inc., 555 Broadway, New York, NY 10012, by arrangement with Andrews and McMeel, a Universal Press Syndicate Company.

12 11 10 9 8 7   8 9/9

02

Printed in the U.S.A.

First Scholastic printing, November 1993

calvin and Hobbes
by WATTERSON

"...H-HELLO? ... ANYB-BODY ??"

ON A CLEAR NIGHT LIKE THIS, YOU REALIZE HOW INCOMPREHENSIBLY VAST THE UNIVERSE REALLY IS.

THERE'S VENUS. THERE'S MARS, AND THERE'S JUPITER.

I WONDER WHAT EARLY MAN MUST'VE THOUGHT AS HE WATCHED THE SKIES.

HE'D SEE HE WAS AN INFINITESIMAL PART OF CREATION, BUT HE'D HAVE NO UNDERSTANDING OF PLANETS OR STARS OR COMETS OR ANYTHING.

IMAGINE HOW BIG AND MYSTERIOUS THE NIGHT WOULD'VE SEEMED TO HIM! I'LL BET HE FELT VERY FRAGILE AND AFRAID, DON'T YOU THINK?

AND I'M STUCK HERE.

I'LL BET THAT'S WHAT HE FELT LIKE! SABER-TOOTH TIGER FOOD!

FROM NOW ON I'M GOING TO STAY INSIDE AT NIGHT AND WATCH T.V.

...HOBBES? HOBBES ??

IS OUR QUICK EXPERIENCE HERE POINTLESS? DOES ANYTHING WE SAY OR DO IN HERE REALLY MATTER? HAVE WE DONE ANYTHING IMPORTANT? HAVE WE BEEN HAPPY? HAVE WE MADE THE MOST OF THESE PRECIOUS FEW FOOTSTEPS??

BAD GUESS.

POOR GENETIC MATERIAL?

NOW WE FIND OURSELVES SOMEWHERE INSIDE THE SQUARE, AND IN THE PROCESS OF WALKING OUT OF IT. SUDDENLY WE REALIZE OUR TIME IN HERE IS FLEETING.

WHAT ON EARTH WOULD MAKE YOU *DO* SOMETHING LIKE THAT?!

LET'S SAY LIFE IS THIS SQUARE OF THE SIDEWALK. WE'RE BORN AT THIS CRACK AND WE DIE AT THAT CRACK.

YOU'VE BEEN HITTING *ROCKS* IN THE *HOUSE?!*

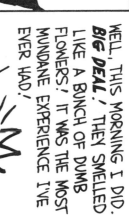

12

THIS MEETING OF THE GET RID OF SLIMY GIRLS CLUB IS NOW IN SESSION! FIRST TIGER HOBBES WILL PRESENT OUR FINANCIAL REPORT.

WAIT, WE DIDN'T SING THE G.R.O.S.S. ANTHEM.

WE SING THAT AT THE *END* OF THE MEETING.

I WANT TO SING IT *NOW*.

WE CAN'T. WE HAVE TO FOLLOW PROPER PROTOCOL! SEE? IT SAYS ON THE AGENDA THAT WE SING THE ANTHEM *LAST*.

OHHOHH GROHOSS ♪ BEST CLUB IN THE COSMOS... ♪

STOP THAT, YOU ANARCHIST!

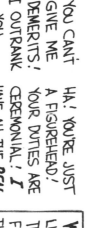

YOU GET TWO DEMERITS FOR SINGING THE CLUB ANTHEM BEFORE IT WAS ON THE AGENDA!

WELL *YOU* GET *FIVE* DEMERITS FOR NOT TAKING OFF YOUR HAT DURING ITS HALLOWED REFRAIN!

YOU CAN'T GIVE ME DEMERITS! I OUTRANK YOU.

HA! YOU'RE JUST A FIGUREHEAD! YOUR DUTIES ARE CEREMONIAL! *I* HAVE ALL THE *REAL* RESPONSIBILITIES!

WHAT?! I'M DICTATOR-FOR-LIFE! I HAVE TEN *TIMES* THE IMPORTANCE OF A LOWLY FIRST TIGER! A *HUNDRED* TIMES! A *MILLION* TIMES!

IF YOU'RE SO IMPORTANT, HOW COME YOU SING THE SOPRANO PART OF OUR ANTHEM?

THAT'S JUST TILL MY VOICE CHANGES!

14

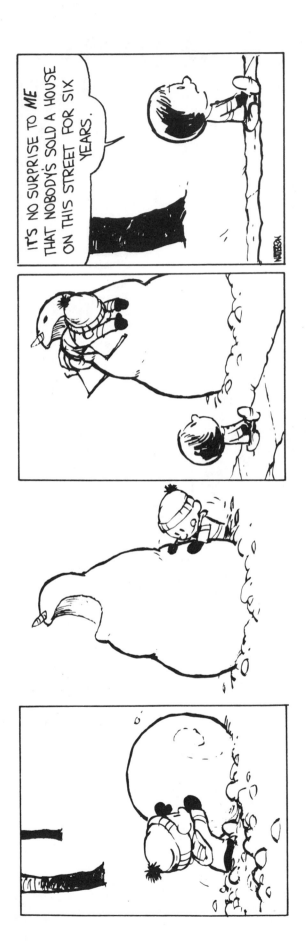

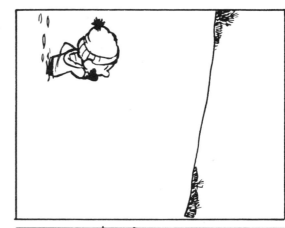

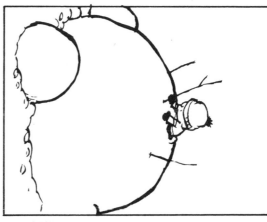

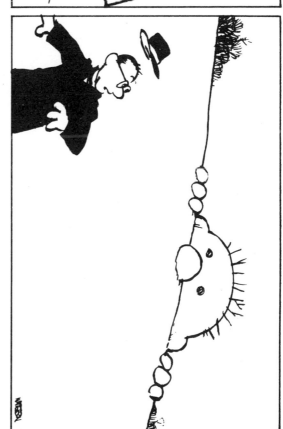

HELP! HELP! MY HEAD SOMEHOW GOT TWISTED COMPLETELY AROUND! I'M FACING BACKWARD!

LOOK! I CAN READ THE TAG ON MY SHIRT! I CAN SEE DOWN MY OWN BACK!

...OH, WAIT. THERE'S MY BELLY BUTTON. I MUST JUST HAVE MY *SHIRT* ON BACKWARD.

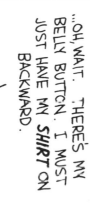

NEVER MIND. I'VE GOT MY HEAD ON STRAIGHT AFTER ALL.

OH, I WOULDN'T GO THAT FAR.

22

LOOK, DAD MADE ME DO MY HOMEWORK!

HE SAID, WHEN I'M OLDER, I'LL DISCOVER THAT THERE ARE FEW PLEASURES GREATER THAN LEARNING.

SO I SAID, FINE, I'LL LEARN WHEN I'M OLDER!

WHAT DID HE SAY?

HE SAID, IF I DIDN'T START CRACKING BOOKS NOW, THIS WOULD BE AS OLD AS I'D GET.

SOUNDS LIKE YOU LEARNED SOMETHING ALREADY.

SEE, HOBBES, WE SHOULDN'T NEED ACCOMPLISHMENTS TO FEEL GOOD ABOUT OURSELVES. SELF-ESTEEM SHOULDN'T BE CONDITIONAL.

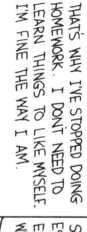

THAT'S WHY I'VE STOPPED DOING HOMEWORK. I DON'T NEED TO LEARN THINGS TO LIKE MYSELF. I'M FINE THE WAY I AM.

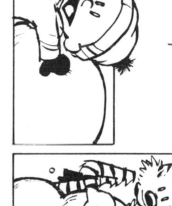

SO THE SECRET TO GOOD SELF-ESTEEM IS TO LOWER YOUR EXPECTATIONS TO THE POINT WHERE THEY'RE ALREADY MET?

RIGHT. WE SHOULD TAKE PRIDE IN OUR MEDIOCRITY.

I THINK THIS SNOWMAN IS GOOD ENOUGH, DON'T YOU?

REMIND ME TO INVEST OVERSEAS.

calvin and Hobbes by WATTERSON

PEOPLE PUSHED TO GET AWAY! THE ELDERLY AND SMALL WERE TRAMPLED UNDERFOOT BY THE ADVANCING HUMAN WALL! LITTLE TIM WAS ON AN ERRAND WITH HIS BROTHER HOWARD. THEY DAWDLED BY THE CANDY SHOP AND BOTH BOYS WERE DEVOURED.

TYRANNOSAURS, THOUGH RARELY SEEN, ARE CERTAINLY STILL AROUND, AND NO ONE KNOWS JUST WHERE OR WHEN THE NEXT ONE WILL BE FOUND.

NGGRR!/ FTH! NNGGRR!

BLOW YOUR NOSE, DEAR.

... EXCEPT ME.

IMAGINE, THEN, THE PANIC CAUSED, THE HORROR AND THE MAYHEM, WHEN THIS MONSTER CAME TO TOWN AND ATE SOME FOLKS THIS A.M.! IT WAS A SIGHT FEW WILL FORGET! HE LUNGED INTO THE CROWD! THE MULTITUDE BECAME UNGLUED! THEIR SCREAMS WERE LONG AND LOUD!

A CAMERA CREW FROM CHANNEL THREE ARRIVED IN TOWN TO GIVE A LIVE REPORT. AT THIS THEY FAILED, BECAUSE THEY DIDN'T LIVE. AT LAST THE MENACE ATE HIS FILL. THE BIG TYRANNOSAUR STOMPED AWAY TO PARTS UNKNOWN WHERE HE HAD LIVED BEFORE.

EIGHTY MILLION YEARS AGO, BACK IN THE LATE CRETACEOUS, LIVED THE GREAT TYRANNOSAUR, A FEARSOME AND PREDACIOUS THEROPOD OF MONSTROUS SIZE! HE WEIGHED SIX TONS OR MORE; HE EPITOMIZED THE CONCEPT OF THE KILLER CARNIVORE!

HIS JAWS HAD TEETH LIKE RAILROAD SPIKES WITH FORE AND AFT SERRATIONS! THIS DENTAL HARDWARE WAS DESIGNED FOR QUICK EVISCERATIONS! WITH THRASHING BITES AND AWFUL ROARS THE T. REX WOULD ATTACK! HE WAS, IT'S CLEAR, A SAVAGE MESOZOIC MANIAC!

HERE WE STAND, PEERING DOWN THE DIZZYING DEPTHS OF DOOM DROP! DO WE TURN AROUND AND RETREAT TO THE STUPEFYING SECURITY OF HOME AND HEARTH?

MOM AND DAD DRIVE ME CRAZY.

OR DO WE BRAVE THE DESCENT, RISK DEMISE, AND EXPERIENCE THE FLOOD OF SOMATIC SENSATION THAT SCREAMS WE ARE ALIVE, GLORIOUSLY ALIVE, HOWEVER TEMPORARILY?

THEY DON'T UNDERSTAND **ME** AND I DON'T UNDERSTAND **THEM.** IT'S HOPELESS!

"HOBBES?"

I'M RELATED TO PEOPLE I DON'T RELATE TO.

I THOUGHT THE QUESTION WAS RHETORICAL.

THE OTHER WAY, THOUGH!

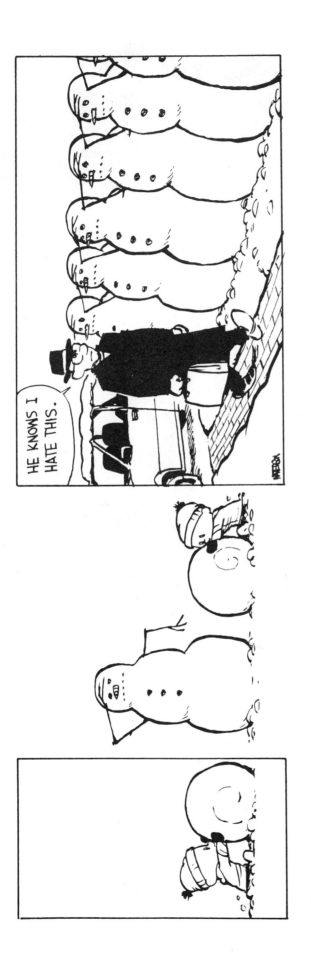

28

29

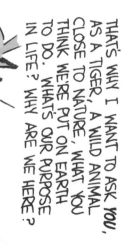

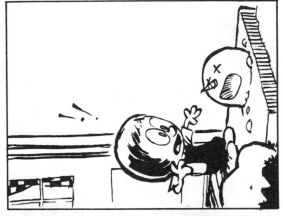

HELLO, IS THIS THE HARDWARE
STORE? YES, I'M WONDERING
IF YOU SELL CATAPULTS.

NO?? WELL, I'M LOOKING FOR
SOMETHING THAT CAN DELIVER
A 50-POUND PAYLOAD OF SNOW
ON A SMALL FEMININE TARGET.
CAN YOU SUGGEST SOMETHING?

HELLO?

I DON'T UNDERSTAND HOW
SOME OF THESE PLACES
STAY IN BUSINESS.

WHAT'S WRONG WITH
EASTER ISLAND?
I *LIKE* EASTER
ISLAND.

37

40

41

42

I SUPPOSE ONE COULD RECOGNIZE A BOY OF DESTINY BY HIS PLANET-AND-STAR UNDERPANTS.

ANOTHER TRENCHANT COMMENT BY A JEALOUS LESSER INTELLECT.

IT'S NOT EASY HAVING A MIND THAT OPERATES ON A HIGHER PLANE THAN EVERYONE ELSE'S! PEOPLE JUST REFUSE TO SEE THAT I'M THE CRUX OF ALL HISTORY, A BOY OF DESTINY!

PEOPLE DON'T REALIZE WHAT A BURDEN IT IS BEING A GENIUS LIKE ME.

I THINK I'M GOING TO STOP INTRODUCING YOU ALTOGETHER.

I WISH YOU HAD SOME CYMBALS TO CRASH AFTER YOU SAID IT.

BUT YOU HAVE TO SAY IT RIGHT. PAUSE A LITTLE AFTER "BOY," AND SAY "DESTINY" A BIT SLOWER AND DEEPER FOR EMPHASIS. SAY IT, "BOY...... OF DESSSTINY," LIKE THAT!

BOY OF DESTINY?!

I WANT TO BE INTRODUCED AS "CALVIN, BOY OF DESTINY."

MOM, FROM NOW ON, I DON'T WANT TO BE INTRODUCED TO PEOPLE AS PLAIN "CALVIN."

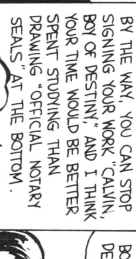

48

DID YOU EVEN READ THE HISTORY CHAPTER I ASSIGNED?

I TRIED TO, MISS WORMWOOD, BUT THE BOOK PUBLISHER DIDN'T USE THE PROPER PRINT FIXATIVE.

NEEDLESS TO SAY, WHEN I PICKED UP THE BOOK, ALL THE LETTERS SLID OFF THE PAGES AND FELL ON THE FLOOR IN A HEAP OF GIBBERISH.

I THINK MY EXCUSES NEED TO BE LESS EXTEMPORANEOUS.

PRINCIPAL

COUNTY LIBRARY? REFERENCE DESK, PLEASE. HELLO? YES, I NEED A WORD DEFINITION.

WELL, THAT'S THE PROBLEM. I DON'T KNOW HOW TO SPELL IT AND I'M NOT ALLOWED TO SAY IT.

COULD YOU JUST RATTLE OFF ALL THE SWEAR WORDS YOU KNOW, AND I'LL STOP YOU WHEN... HELLO??

SEE IF I EVER VOTE FOR THEIR TAX LEVIES.

49

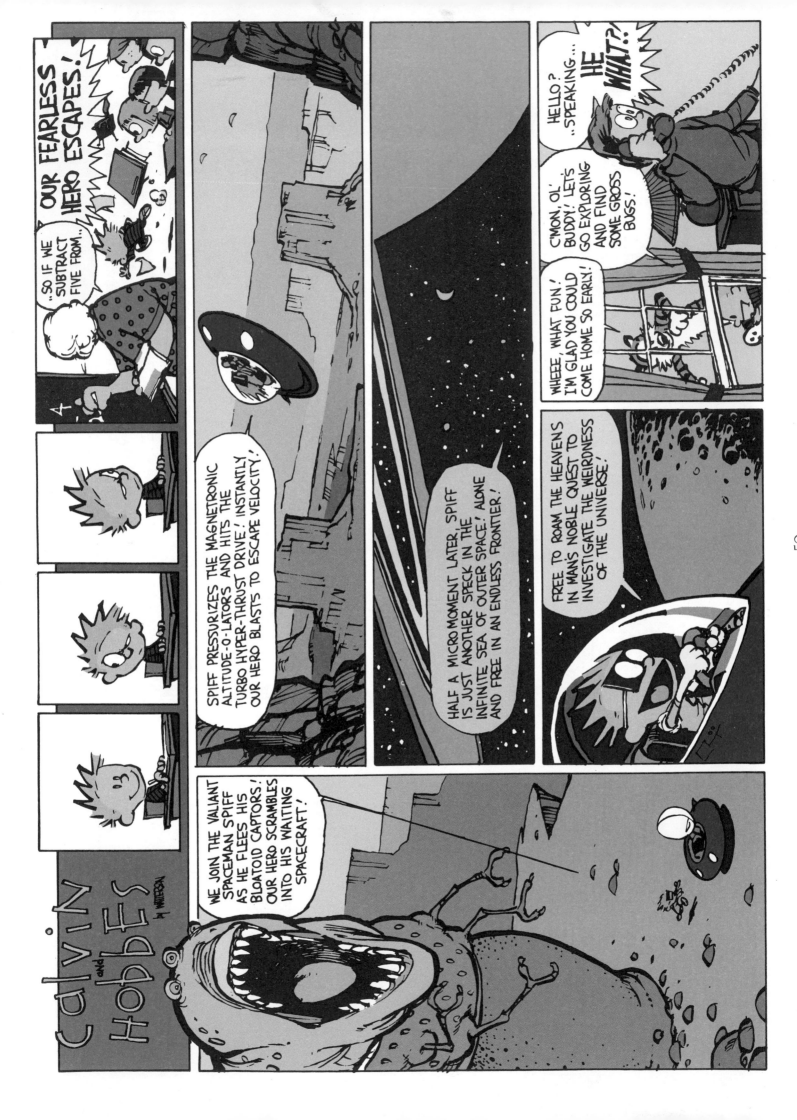

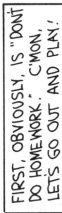

YOUR MOM DIDN'T CARE MUCH ABOUT THE LUNAR SANCTION OF YOUR NO-HOMEWORK POLICY, DID SHE?

HMPH.

WELL, MY HOROSCOPE SAID "*MANY* KEY POLICIES WILL BE IMPLEMENTED," NOT *ALL* OF THEM. BESIDES, IT SAYS TO EXPECT A TURNABOUT IN MY FAVOR. MOM WILL RELENT NEXT TIME FOR SURE.

WHAT ARE YOUR OTHER KEY POLICIES THEN?

NO BATHS, STAY UP LATE, DON'T GO TO SCHOOL... *THESE* ARE THE ONES THAT WILL BE IMPLEMENTED.

MAYBE THE ASTROLOGER WAS LOOKING THROUGH THE WRONG END OF THE TELESCOPE.

C'MON MOON, DO YOUR STUFF!

I THOUGHT I TOLD YOU TO TAKE YOUR BATH.

SORRY, MOM. YOU HAVE NO SAY IN THIS.

YOU'RE IN FOR A SURPRISE, BUSTER.

CIRCUMSTANCES ARE GOING TO TURN IN MY FAVOR! THAT'S WHAT MY HOROSCOPE SAYS!

ALL HUMAN AFFAIRS ARE DETERMINED BY STARS AND PLANETS, AND TODAY THEY SAY MY KEY POLICIES WILL BE IMPLEMENTED. THAT MEANS NO BATH AND NO BEDTIME!

BY GOLLY, IT'S NOT GOOD TO THWART THE INTENTIONS OF THE UNIVERSE!

FATE JUST ISN'T WHAT IT USED TO BE.

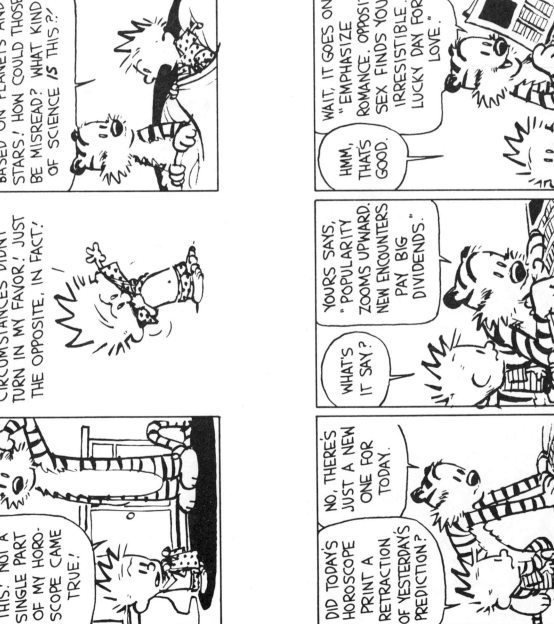

SO SUSIE DIDN'T KISS YOU TODAY?

NOPE! IN FACT, AFTER I PUT A WORM IN HER HAIR, SHE KNOCKED ME DOWN AND KICKED ME IN THE SHINS!

THAT DOESN'T SOUND LIKE ZOOMING POPULARITY.

NOPE! MY HOROSCOPE WAS COMPLETELY WRONG AGAIN! THE PLANETS OBVIOUSLY HAVE NO INFLUENCE ON ME!

WHAT A RELIEF TO KNOW MY LIFE ISN'T CONTROLLED BY OUTSIDE FORCES! I'M THE MASTER OF MY OWN FATE!

..TO A POINT, OF COURSE. THE PAPER SHOULD PRINT MOM'S DAILY PREDICTIONS. *THOSE* SURE COME TRUE.

I'VE BEEN THINKING ABOUT THIS ASTROLOGY STUFF.

EVERYONE WANTS TO KNOW WHAT THE FUTURE HOLDS, BUT YOU JUST HAVE TO WAIT 'TIL IT HAPPENS.

SO REALLY, THE BEST PREPARATION FOR THE FUTURE IS TO TAKE THE PRESENT AND..

WHOOP! AUUGHH!!

..THINK ABOUT WHAT YOU'RE DOING?

NO, GET YOURSELF A GOOD LUCK CHARM, MAN, HERE COMES *ANOTHER* BATH!

FOR SCHOOL, WE'RE SUPPOSED TO WRITE A PARAGRAPH ABOUT WHAT OUR DADS DO.

"DAD: THE PARAGRAPH." CATCHY TITLE, HUH?

"WHAT DOES MY DAD DO? MOSTLY, HE GETS ON MY NERVES. THE END."

YOU MAY GET A POINT FOR SUCCINCTNESS. WELL WHAT ELSE IS THERE TO SAY?!

I THINK WE NEED A NEW POLICY IN THIS HOUSE. AND WHAT'S THAT?

FROM NOW ON, WHENEVER YOU TELL ME THINGS, I DON'T WANT TO HEAR ANY REASONS, EXPLANATIONS, SUBTLETY OR CONTEXT.

I JUST WANT TEN-SECOND SOUND BITES, OK?

SO MUCH FOR *THAT* POLICY.

AND HIS FEET! THEY AREN'T THE SAME SIZE! THEY FACE OUT SIDEWAYS. HOW CAN CALVIN STAND UP? WHO KNOWS?

GEE, IT WAS GETTING PRETTY GOOD AT THE END.

I HATE DRAWING! WHAT A WASTE OF TIME!

AAUGHH! CALVIN'S HANDS ARE BALLS WITH STICKS IN THEM! HE DOESN'T EVEN HAVE THE RIGHT NUMBER OF FINGERS! WHERE ARE HIS THUMBS??

RRRRGGHH!

Calvin and Hobbes by WATTERSON

HIS NOSTRILS ARE ON THE FRONT OF HIS NOSE LIKE A **PIG**! HIS EARS ARE JUST FLAPS ON HIS HEAD! AND WHAT'S THIS STUFF ON TOP? IS THAT SUPPOSED TO BE *HAIR*??

HERE WE GO! HA HA!

WHAT A HORRIBLE FATE! HIS EYES DON'T EVEN POINT THE SAME DIRECTION! EACH EYE SEES A DIFFERENT VIEW!

HOW CAN HE BE SAVED?? WHAT CAN BE DONE??

WHAT'S GONE WRONG? HE'S A CRUDE BLACK OUTLINE BARELY CONTAINING GARISH COLOR!

OH NO! LOOK AT POOR CALVIN!

LOOK AT HIS MORONIC EXPRESSION! HIS FACE REVEALS NO SPARK OF INTELLIGENCE! CALVIN IS DEVOID OF REALITY AND SUBSTANCE!

68

69

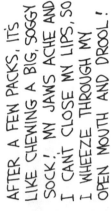

OH BOY, THE NEW ISSUE OF "CHEWING"!

YOU GET A MAGAZINE?

WOW, THIS LOOKS GREAT! "SPECIAL SUGARLESS GUM ISSUE - CHOOSING AN ARTIFICIAL SWEETENER THAT'S RIGHT FOR YOU .... TONGUE EXERCISES FOR BIGGER BUBBLES .... RAD FASHION KNEEPADS FOR WALKING AND CHEWING .... PLUS AN INTERVIEW WITH BAZOOKA JOE!"

SEE, IT'S ALL TARGET MARKETING! ADVERTISERS DON'T WASTE THEIR TIME ON MASS AUDIENCES ANY MORE. THEY FIND YOUR SPECIAL INTEREST AND THEY NAIL YOU!

AS IF ADVERTISING WASN'T INTRUSIVE ENOUGH BEFORE.

OOH, THE '92 SPEARMINTS ARE OUT! I GOTTA GET TO A STORE!

I CAN'T BELIEVE THERE'S A MAGAZINE FOR GUM CHEWERS.

HECK, THERE MUST BE A DOZEN SUCH MAGAZINES.

EACH APPEALS TO A DIFFERENT FACTION. "CHEWING" IS HIGH-GLOSS, LITERATE AND SOPHISTICATED. "GUM ACTION" GOES FOR THE GONZO CHEWERS. "CHEWERS ILLUSTRATED" AIMS AT VINTAGE GUM COLLECTORS, AND SO ON!

EACH ONE ENCOURAGES YOU TO THINK YOU BELONG TO AN ELITE CLIQUE, SO ADVERTISERS CAN APPEAL TO YOUR EGO AND GET YOU TO CULTIVATE AN IMAGE THAT SETS YOU APART FROM THE CROWD. IT'S THE DIVIDE AND CONQUER TRICK.

I WONDER WHATEVER HAPPENED TO THE MELTING POT.

THERE'S NO MONEY IN IT.

Panel 1:
HERE'S AN INTERESTING ARTICLE. THE TOP FIVE GUM BRANDS ARE COMPARED IN TERMS OF FLAVOR RETENTION, ELASTICITY, BUBBLE CAPACITY AND CHEWING REBOUND.

Panel 2:
THE COMPUTER GRAPH SHOWS THE RESULTS, COMPENSATING FOR VARIOUS SALIVA ACIDITIES. IF YOU KNOW YOUR pH, THIS REALLY HELPS YOU CHOOSE THE PROPER GUM FOR YOUR CHEWING STYLE.

Panel 3:
WHAT KIND OF NUT WOULD **CARE** ABOUT ALL THIS?!

EVERYONE! THIS IS HARD DATA! IT LETS YOU QUANTIFY YOUR ENJOYMENT!

Panel 4:
I THOUGHT FUN WAS SUPPOSED TO BE *FUN.*

WELL *I* PREFER TO TRUST THE EXPERTS.

Panel 5:
HERE'S AN AD FOR A NEW GUM CALLED "HYPERBUBBLE," AND IT SAYS, "IF YOU'RE NOT CHEWING HYPERBUBBLE, YOU MIGHT AS WELL BE CHEWING YOUR CUD." OOH, GREAT COPY!

Panel 6:
GOSH. AM I COOL ENOUGH TO CHEW HYPERBUBBLE? MAYBE I'M **NOT**! MAYBE IF YOU CHEW HYPERBUBBLE, YOU *BECOME* COOL!

Panel 7:
OR MAYBE IF YOU CHEW IT, EVERYONE **ASSUMES** YOU'RE COOL, SO IT DOESN'T MATTER IF YOU ARE OR NOT! WHAT DO YOU THINK? SHOULD I BUY SOME?

Panel 8:
IF YOUR EMOTIONAL SECURITY DEPENDS ON SATISFYING A NEED YOU DIDN'T HAVE UNTIL YOU READ THE AD, GO AHEAD.

I THINK I WILL! BOY, I'M GLAD I GET THIS MAGAZINE!

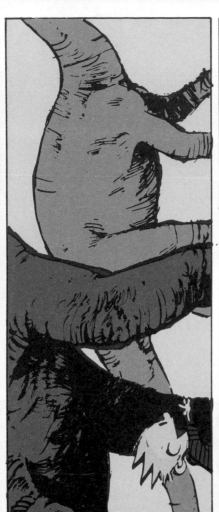

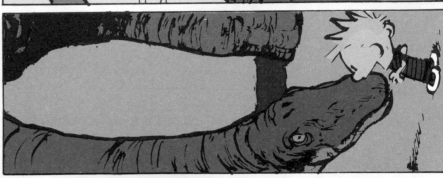

AS I, THE MANIACAL TYRANT, LOOK DOWN UPON MY PATHETIC SUBJECTS,...

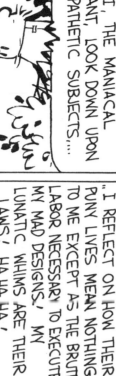

"I REFLECT ON HOW THEIR PUNY LIVES MEAN NOTHING TO ME EXCEPT AS THE BRUTE LABOR NECESSARY TO EXECUTE MY MAD DESIGNS! MY LUNATIC WHIMS ARE THEIR LAWS! HA HA HA!"

I THOUGHT I TOLD YOU TO GATHER THE TRASH.

BEING A PARENT MUST BE NICE.

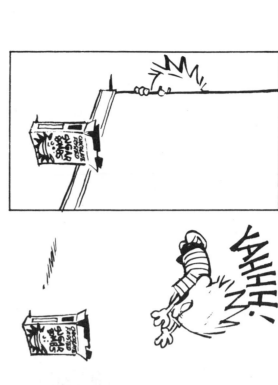

VAHHH!

RRGGHH

MUNCH MUNCH MUNCH

YOU'RE RIGHT. FOOD *DOES* TASTE BETTER THIS WAY.

I'VE GOT TO STOP READING THOSE DUMB ADVICE COLUMNS.

* CLICK *

ACK! OOF! UGH!

... SO PLEASE LEAVE A MESSAGE AT THE SOUND OF THE CLICK.

SHOVE

HELLO, WE ARE UNABLE TO COME TO THE PHONE RIGHT NOW...

A PERSON CAN'T BE A DOORMAT UNLESS HE ALLOWS HIMSELF TO BE ONE! I REFUSE TO BUDGE!

Outta my way, Twinky.

RINGG.. RINNG

THAT'S WHAT'S *IMPORTANT!*

200 B.C. ?!

"BEFORE CALVIN."

OUR COUNTRY WAS FOUNDED A VERY LONG TIME AGO, ROUGHLY AROUND 200 B.C.

IT'S A LOT MORE FUN TO BLAME THINGS THAN TO FIX THEM.

AN INGENIOUSLY SELF-FULFILLING PLAN.

THEN, WHEN EVERYTHING GOES DOWN THE TUBES, I CAN SAY THE SYSTEM DOESN'T WORK AND JUSTIFY MY FURTHER LACK OF PARTICIPATION.

THAT WAY I CAN COMPLAIN THAT THE GOVERNMENT DOESN'T REPRESENT ME.

WHEN I GROW UP, I'M NOT GOING TO READ THE NEWSPAPER AND I'M NOT GOING TO FOLLOW COMPLEX ISSUES AND I'M NOT GOING TO VOTE.

Calvin and Hobbes WATTERSON

IT'S TRUE, HOBBES, IGNORANCE *IS* BLISS!

BUT IF YOU'RE WILLFULLY STUPID, YOU DON'T KNOW ANY BETTER, SO YOU CAN KEEP DOING WHATEVER YOU LIKE!

THE SECRET TO HAPPINESS IS SHORT-TERM, STUPID SELF-INTEREST!

ONCE YOU KNOW THINGS, YOU START SEEING PROBLEMS EVERYWHERE...

...AND ONCE YOU SEE PROBLEMS, YOU FEEL LIKE YOU OUGHT TO TRY TO FIX THEM...

...AND FIXING PROBLEMS ALWAYS SEEMS TO REQUIRE PERSONAL CHANGE...

...AND CHANGE MEANS DOING THINGS THAT AREN'T FUN! I SAY PHOOEY TO THAT!

WE'RE HEADING FOR THAT CLIFF!

I DON'T WANT TO KNOW ABOUT IT.

WAAAUGGHHH!

I'M NOT SURE I CAN STAND SO MUCH BLISS.

CAREFUL! WE DON'T WANT TO LEARN ANYTHING FROM THIS.

IF YOU ASK *ME*, THESE ASSIGNMENTS DON'T TEACH YOU HOW TO WRITE. THEY TEACH YOU HOW TO *HATE* TO WRITE.

DEADLINES, RULES, HOW TO DO IT, GRADES... HOW CAN YOU BE CREATIVE WHEN SOMEONE'S BREATHING DOWN YOUR NECK?

I GUESS YOU SHOULD TRY NOT TO THINK ABOUT THE END RESULT TOO MUCH AND JUST HAVE FUN WITH THE PROCESS OF CREATING.

EVERY TIME I DO THAT, I END UP IN THE SCHOOL PSYCHOLOGIST'S OFFICE.

WELL, MAYBE NOT *THAT* MUCH FUN.

SAY, *I'VE* GOT AN IDEA!

FOR YOUR STORY?

NO, I THOUGHT OF A WAY I WON'T HAVE TO WRITE ONE!

OH NO.

HOP IN THE TIME MACHINE, HOBBES! WE'RE GOING A FEW HOURS INTO THE FUTURE! I'LL HAVE FINISHED MY STORY BY THEN, SO WE'LL JUST PICK IT UP AND BRING IT BACK TO THE PRESENT! THAT WAY, I WON'T HAVE TO WRITE IT!

SOMETHING DOESN'T MAKE SENSE HERE, AND I THINK IT'S ME SITTING IN THIS BOX.

RELAX! WE'LL BE BACK AS SOON AS WE GO.

88

89

Calvin and Hobbes
by WATTERSON
CALVIN, THE COMMERCIAL AIRLINE PILOT, DECIDES NOT TO FLY TO ST. LOUIS AS SCHEDULED!
CALVIN DOESN'T *WANT* TO SEE ST. LOUIS! CALVIN WANTS TO SEE THE *GRAND CANYON*!
...UP CLOSE!
TOURISTS ON THE RIM WAVE TO CALVIN'S SCREAMING PASSENGERS AS THE JET ROARS INTO THE GORGE!
WHAT A VIEW! IT'S AN EXPERIENCE NONE WILL FORGET! EVERYONE WILL BE GLAD LATER THAT CALVIN TOOK THIS SCENIC DETOUR!
IF *I* WAS DRIVING, THAT'S WHERE WE'D GO.
WELL YOU'RE *NOT* DRIVING, AND ARIZONA IS *NOT* ON THE WAY TO THE GROCERY STORE.

ALLO? EEZ THEES DER POOBLIC LAHBRORRY? YAH?

I EM BEEG EEMPORTANT REZEARCHER OOND I REQUIRE ENGLISH VOOLGAR ZYNONYMS FOR DISGUSTINK BODY VUNKTIONS, YAH?

ALLO? ALLO?

NO LUCK?

THOSE LIBRARIANS ARE A SHARP BUNCH.

THIS TOWN JUST AIN'T BIG ENOUGH FER THE BOTH OF US!

YEP, I RECKON WE'LL HAVE TO ANNEX PART O' THE COUNTY!

MOM WON'T LET US PLAY WITH GUNS.

I GET TO BE THE ZONING BOARD!

MAYBE YOU SHOULDN'T USE CHOCOLATE MILK.

I TRIED COLA, BUT THE BUBBLES WENT UP MY NOSE.

...AND BY THE END OF MY *THIRD* BOWL, I USUALLY FEEL SICK.

THE PLEASURE OF MY *FIRST* BOWL IS DIMINISHED BY THE ANTICIPATION OF FUTURE BOWLS...

AHHH, ANOTHER BOWL OF CHOCOLATE FROSTED SUGAR BOMBS! THE SECOND BOWL IS ALWAYS THE BEST!

FORTUNATELY, THAT'S ALL I HAVE THE PATIENCE FOR.

THIS IS A SOUND BITE! THIS IS ENTERTAINMENT! THIS IS SENSATIONALISM!

YOU CALL THIS *NEWS*?! *THIS* ISN'T INFORMATIVE!

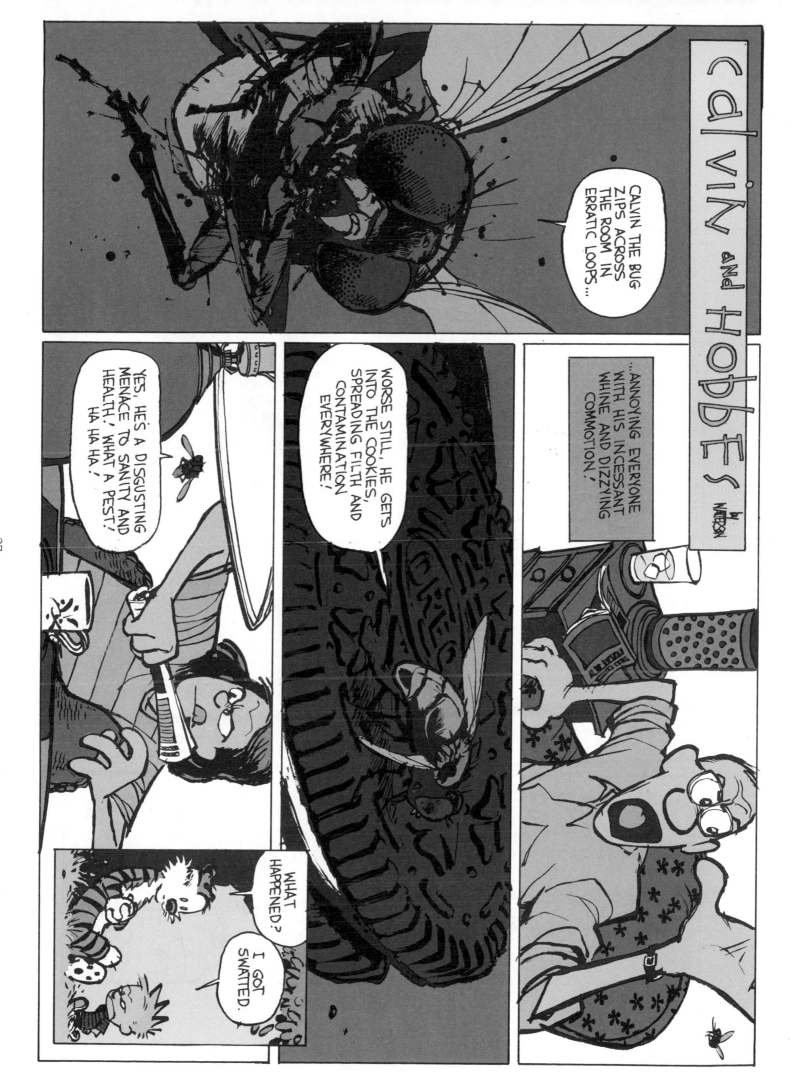

FINE ART IS DEAD, HOBBES. NOBODY UNDERSTANDS IT. NOBODY LIKES IT. NOBODY SEES IT. IT'S IRRELEVANT IN TODAY'S CULTURE.

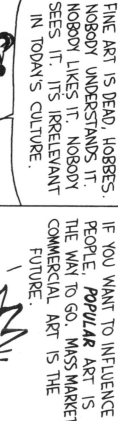

IF YOU WANT TO INFLUENCE PEOPLE, *POPULAR* ART IS THE WAY TO GO. MASS MARKET COMMERCIAL ART IS THE FUTURE.

BESIDES, IT'S THE ONLY WAY TO MAKE SERIOUS MONEY AND THAT'S WHAT'S IMPORTANT ABOUT BEING AN ARTIST.

SO WHAT KIND OF SCULPTURE ARE YOU MAKING?

PLEASE! IT'S NOT "SCULPTURE," IT'S "COLLECTIBLE FIGURINES."

SEE, THE PROBLEM WITH FINE ART IS THAT IT'S SUPPOSED TO EXPRESS ORIGINAL TRUTHS.

BUT WHO LIKES ORIGINALITY AND TRUTH?! NOBODY! LIFE'S HARD ENOUGH WITHOUT IT! ONLY AN IDIOT WOULD *PAY* FOR IT!

BUT *POPULAR ART* KNOWS THE CUSTOMER IS ALWAYS RIGHT! PEOPLE WANT MORE OF WHAT THEY ALREADY **KNOW** THEY LIKE, SO POPULAR ART GIVES IT TO 'EM!

AND HOW **ARE** THE MOVIE SEQUELS THIS SUMMER?

GREAT! MAN, THERE'S NOTHING I HATE MORE THAN PAYING FIVE BUCKS AND HAVING TO DEAL WITH SOME NEW PLOT.

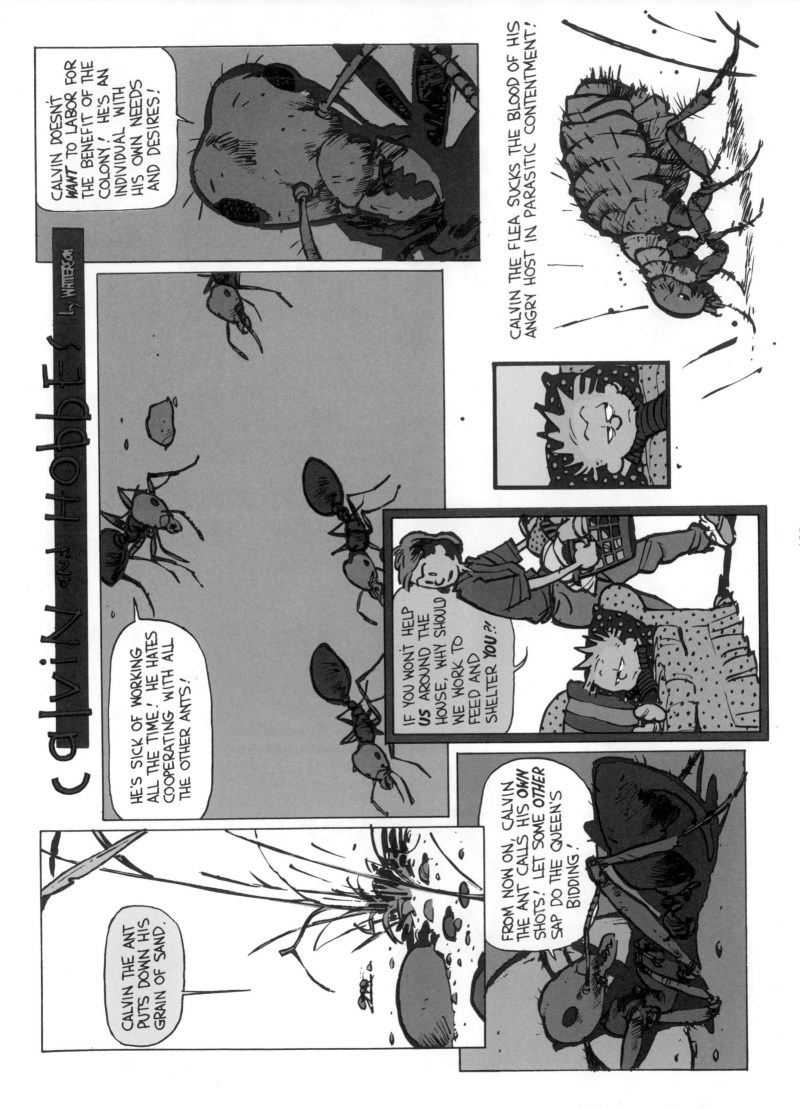

102

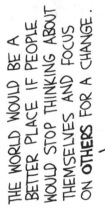

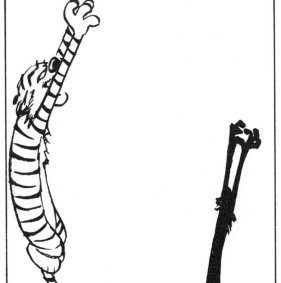

Calvin and Hobbes
by WATTERSON
AAAAAAAAAAAAAAAAAA
MM.. I DON'T THINK SO.
OH, C'MON. I'M RIGHT HERE.

113

HOLY SCHLA*MOLY*, ISN'T THERE A COP SHOW ON WHERE THEY TALK LIKE REAL PEOPLE?

SHHH.

AY, BUT HEAR YOU THIS, I'LL SOON KNOW THY BUSINESS. GET THEE GONE, WASTREL!

BY MY TROTH, I AM OFF.

THOU DOST WRONG ME! FAITH, I KNOW NOT WHERE I WANDER. METHINKS THE MOST CAPRICIOUS ZEPHYR HATH MORE DESIGN THAN I. BUT LO: DO NOT DETAIN ME, FOR I AM RESOLV'D TO QUIT THIS PLACE FORTHWITH.

WHITHER GOEST THOU, YOUNG ROGUE? CAN THERE YET REMAIN SOME VILLANY THOU HAST NOT COMMITTED?

LOOK AT THE GREAT COMMITTEE THAT DREW *THIS* ISSUE!

GOSH, AND I KEEP BUYING BONDS.

OF COURSE, THEY'RE SO CHEAPLY PRINTED YOU HAVE TO PRESERVE THEM IN PLASTIC BAGS, BUT IT'S A SMALL INVESTMENT FOR SUCH A HUGE GUARANTEED RETURN.

SURE! THAT WAY THEY'RE *ALL* COLLECTOR ITEMS! THESE WILL BE WORTH BILLIONS OF DOLLARS SOME DAY!

THE BEST THING ABOUT CAPTAIN STEROID COMIC BOOKS IS THAT EVERY ISSUE IS NUMBER ONE.

EVERY ISSUE??

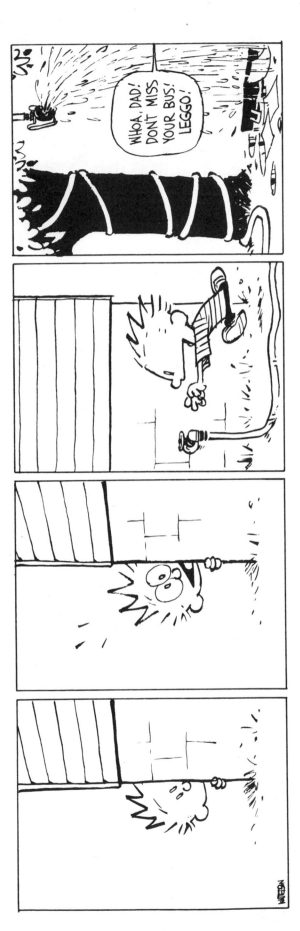

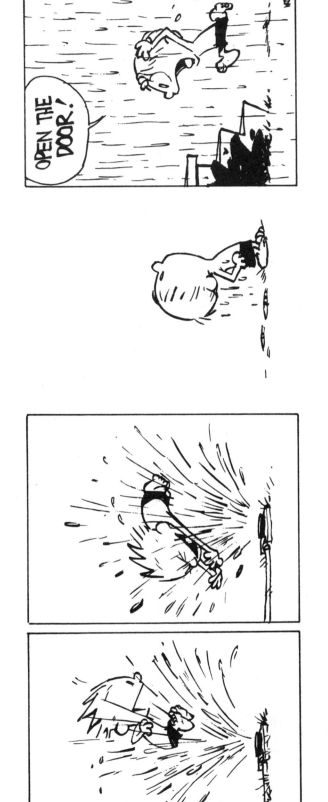

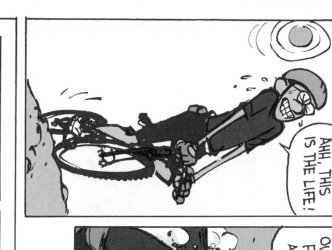

OH, GREATEST OF THE MASS MEDIA, THANK YOU FOR ELEVATING EMOTION, REDUCING THOUGHT, AND STIFLING IMAGINATION.

THANK YOU FOR THE ARTIFICIALITY OF QUICK SOLUTIONS AND FOR THE INSIDIOUS MANIPULATION OF HUMAN DESIRES FOR COMMERCIAL PURPOSES.

THIS BOWL OF LUKEWARM TAPIOCA REPRESENTS MY BRAIN. I OFFER IT IN HUMBLE SACRIFICE. BESTOW THY FLICKERING LIGHT FOREVER.

YOU KNOW WHAT I'VE DISCOVERED?

WHAT?

A LITTLE RUDENESS AND DISRESPECT CAN ELEVATE A MEANINGLESS INTERACTION TO A BATTLE OF WILLS AND ADD DRAMA TO AN OTHERWISE DULL DAY.

OH, THAT'S GOOD TO KNOW.

IF YOU WEREN'T SUCH A MUTTONHEAD, YOU MIGHT HAVE THOUGHT OF IT YOURSELF!

SEE?? YOU PROVED MY POINT!

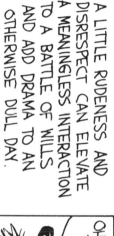

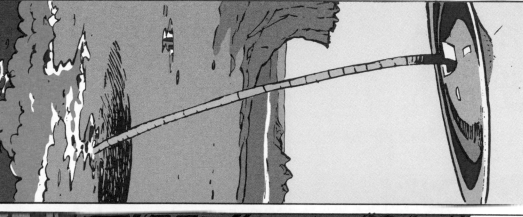

THE ALIENS CAME FROM A FAR DISTANT WORLD IN A LARGE YELLOW SHIP THAT BLINKED AS IT TWIRLED. IT ROUNDED THE MOON, AND ENTERED OUR SKY. WE KNEW THEY HAD COME BUT WE DIDN'T KNOW WHY.

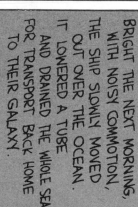

BRIGHT THE NEXT MORNING, WITH NOISY COMMOTION, THE SHIP SLOWLY MOVED OUT OVER THE OCEAN. IT LOWERED A TUBE AND DRAINED THE WHOLE SEA FOR TRANSPORT BACK HOME TO THEIR GALAXY.

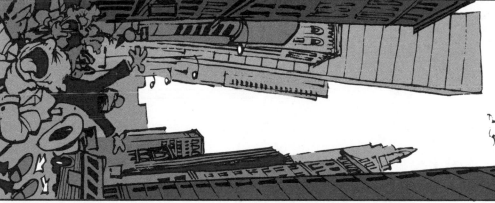

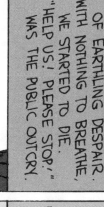

THE TUBE THEN SUCKED UP THE CLOUDS AND THE AIR, CAUSING NO SMALL AMOUNT OF EARTHLING DESPAIR. WITH NOTHING TO BREATHE, WE STARTED TO DIE. "HELP US! PLEASE STOP!" WAS THE PUBLIC OUTCRY.

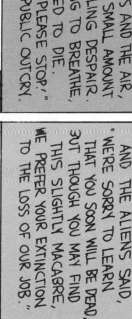

A HATCH OPENED UP AND THE ALIENS SAID, "WE'RE SORRY TO LEARN THAT YOU SOON WILL BE DEAD. BUT THOUGH YOU MAY FIND THIS SLIGHTLY MACABRE, WE PREFER YOUR EXTINCTION TO THE LOSS OF OUR JOB."

THAT'S MY SCIENCE FICTION STORY. THINK IT'S TOO FAR-FETCHED?

NOT ENOUGH, REALLY.

WHEE HEE HEE

RUN FOR YOUR LIFE! THERE'S A MILLION ANGRY HORNETS COMING!

SPLOOSH!!

THEY'RE INSANE WITH RAGE! THEY'LL STING ANYONE IN THEIR PATH! LOUSY BUGS!

WHAT ARE THEY MAD ABOUT?

OH, WHAT AN AWFUL THING I DID! HOW I REGRET IT NOW! I HEREBY RESOLVE TO CHANGE MY EVIL WAYS! OH REMORSE, REMORSE!

I'VE BEEN THROWING ROCKS AT THEIR NEST ALL MORNING.

MY PENITENT SINNER SHTICK NEEDS WORK.

A *REAL* FRIEND WOULDN'T TAKE *THEIR SIDE!*

129

I FEEL I HAVE AN OBLIGATION TO KEEP A JOURNAL OF MY THOUGHTS.

OH?

BEING A GENIUS, MY IDEAS ARE NATURALLY MORE IMPORTANT AND INTERESTING THAN OTHER PEOPLE'S, SO I FIGURE THE WORLD WOULD BENEFIT FROM A RECORD OF MY MENTAL ACTIVITIES.

HOW PHILANTHROPIC OF YOU.

WELL, THE WORLD ISN'T GOING TO GET IT CHEAP.

SO WHAT ARE YOU WRITING TODAY?

I COULDN'T REALLY THINK OF ANYTHING, SO I'M DRAWING SOME MARTIANS ATTACKING INDIANAPOLIS.

TA DA DA DAAAAA! I'M STUPENDOUS MAN!

KAPWINNNGGG!

VIRTUAL REALITY HAS NOTHING ON CALVIN.

MOM WANTS ME TO TRY AN EXPERIMENT TONIGHT.

SHE SAYS THE MONSTERS UNDER MY BED MAY NEED ME TO *THINK* ABOUT THEM TO EXIST.

HER THEORY IS THAT IF I JUST DON'T THINK ABOUT THEM, THEY'LL GO AWAY.

"...OF COURSE, THAT IDEA OF BEING DRAGGED UNDER THE BED AND DEVOURED BY MONSTERS HAS A WAY OF GRIPPING THE MIND.

AND IT'S NOT LIKE MOM AND DAD GO AWAY WHEN I STOP THINKING ABOUT *THEM*.

ATTENTION ALL MONSTERS: I AM NOW GOING TO STOP THINKING ABOUT YOU!

MOMMMM!

ADMIT IT, YOU *LIED* TO US!

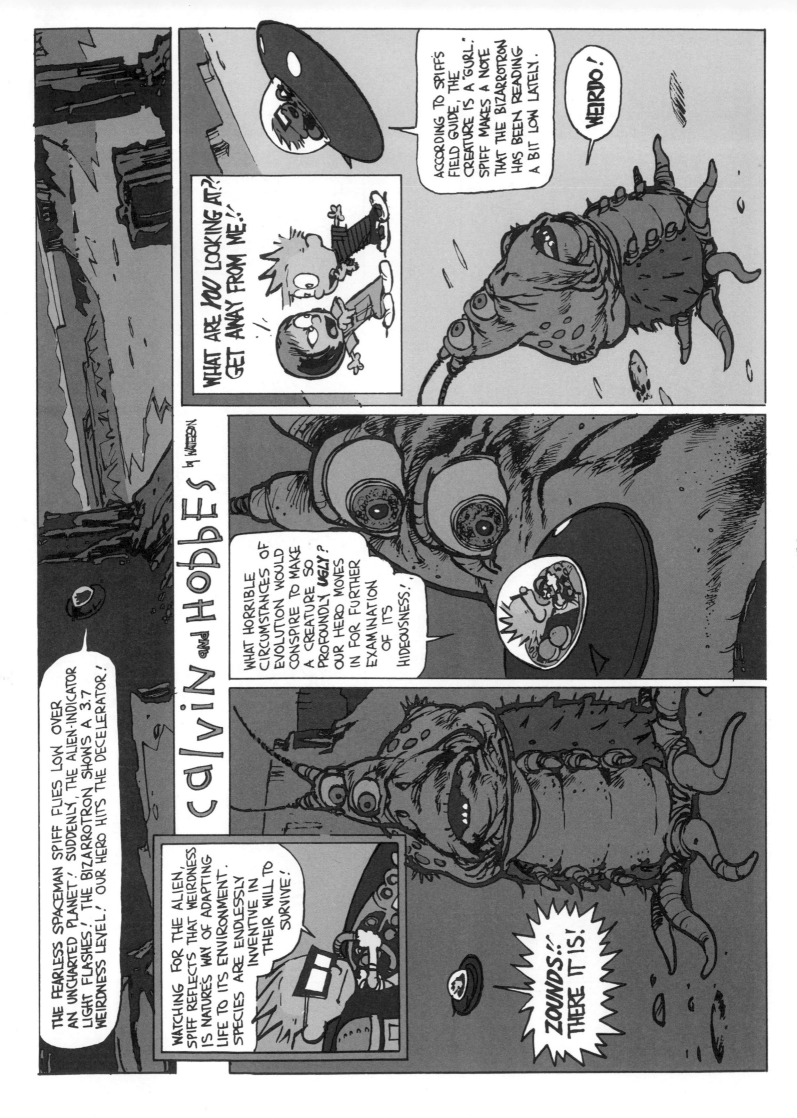

138

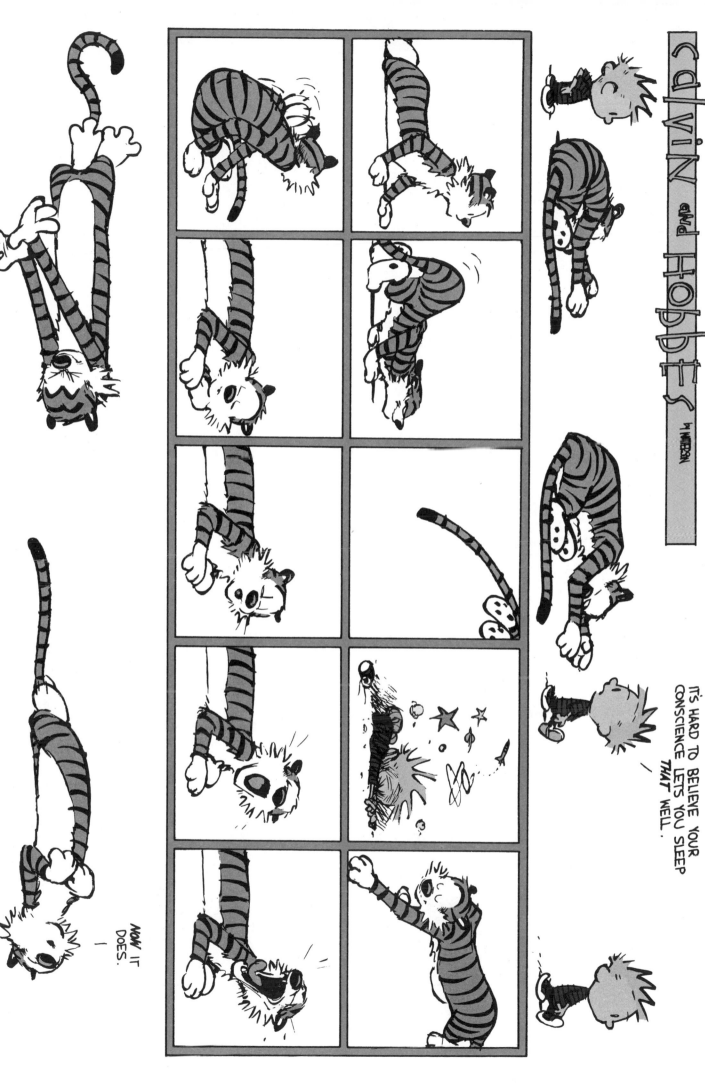

144

145

146

ON THE OFF-CHANCE I DECIDE TO DO SOMETHING RESPONSIBLE WITH MY LIFE, I'LL NEED TO ESTABLISH A FICTITIOUS CHILDHOOD.

WHY DO YOU WANT A PICTURE LIKE *THAT*?

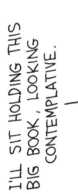

I'LL SIT HOLDING THIS BIG BOOK, LOOKING CONTEMPLATIVE.

HERE, TAKE A PICTURE OF ME, OK?

SURE.

WAIT, LET ME COMB MY HAIR AND PUT ON A TIE.

IS THIS EVEN LEGAL?

FOR EXAMPLE, I'VE CLEARED OFF THIS CORNER OF MY BED. TAKE A PICTURE OF ME HERE, BUT CROP OUT ALL THE MESS AROUND ME, SO IT LOOKS LIKE I KEEP MY ROOM TIDY.

THEY THINK THE CAMERA IS A DISPASSIONATE MACHINE THAT RECORDS ONLY FACTS, BUT REALLY, CAMERAS LIE ALL THE TIME! SELECT THE FACTS AND YOU MANIPULATE THE TRUTH!

THIS IS WHAT I LIKE ABOUT PHOTOGRAPHY. PEOPLE THINK CAMERAS ALWAYS TELL THE TRUTH.

OK, THERE'S A PICTURE OF ME LOOKING WELL-ADJUSTED AND PLAYING SPORTS. THAT OUGHT TO DO IT.

YOU HATE SPORTS.

YEAH, BUT PEOPLE BELIEVE WHAT THEY SEE, AND NOW WE'VE GOT A PHOTOGRAPHIC DOCUMENT OF A FAKE CHILDHOOD READY FOR ANY FUTURE BIOGRAPHICAL NEEDS I MAY HAVE!

PRETTY SHREWD PLANNING, HUH?

EXCEPT FOR ONE DETAIL. SUPPOSE THE PHOTOGRAPHER DOESN'T KEEP QUIET?

YOU DRIVE A HARD BARGAIN, FLEA-BAIT.

OOH, NOW MAGGOT-MAN IS ABOUT TO REVEAL HIS SECRET IDENTITY TO AMAZON-BABE!

I'M A SIMPLE MAN, HOBBES.

YOU?? YESTERDAY YOU WANTED A NUCLEAR POWERED CAR THAT COULD TURN INTO A JET WITH LASER-GUIDED HEAT-SEEKING MISSILES!

I'M A SIMPLE MAN WITH COMPLEX TASTES.

Calvin and Hobbes by Watterson

WUMP

I NEED TO MAKE FRIENDS WITH SOME LESS TERRITORIAL ANIMALS.

YOU HAVE A QUESTION, CALVIN?

MORE OF A STATEMENT, REALLY.

I JUST WANT TO SAY THAT EDUCATION IS OUR MOST IMPORTANT INVESTMENT IN THE FUTURE, AND IT'S SCANDALOUS HOW LITTLE OUR EDUCATORS ARE PAID!

OK, HANDS UP. WHO ELSE DIDN'T DO THE HOMEWORK FOR TODAY?

ACTUALLY, I'D LIKE TO SEE MORE TEACHERS OUT ON THE STREETS.

You're dead at recess, Twinky.

YOU DON'T SCARE ME, MOE.

THIS IS JUST YOUR CLUMSY WAY OF COPING WITH THE FACT THAT I'M A GENIUS AND YOU'RE STILL STRUGGLING WITH THE CONCEPT OF WALKING ERECT.

POW!

THE TRUTH WILL SET YOUR TEETH FREE.

I THINK MOM LETTERED IN SHOT PUT HER JUNIOR YEAR.

I HATE SCHOOL! I'M NOT GOING TO SCHOOL EVER AGAIN! I REFUSE!

MY DISSERTATION ON ETHICS WAS *VERY* WELL RECEIVED.

GOSH, I NEVER REALIZED KILLING WAS SO GROUNDED IN THE LIBERAL ARTS.

ATTACKING RUNNING ANIMALS INVOLVES A LOT OF PHYSICS. THERE'S VELOCITY, GRAVITY AND LAWS OF MOTION, NOT TO MENTION ALL THE BIOLOGY WE HAVE TO KNOW. THEN THERE'S THE ARTISTIC EXPRESSION OF IT ALL, AND A LOT MORE!

HEY!

I HATE GOING TO SCHOOL. I WISH *I* WAS A TIGER. TIGERS DON'T NEED TO KNOW ANYTHING.

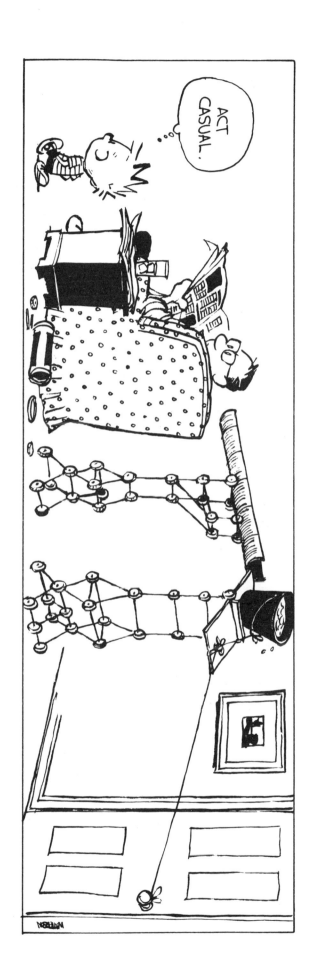

153

154

THAT WAY YOU KNOW EVENTS HAVE BEEN PACKAGED FOR YOUR CONVENIENCE! I LIKE A NARRATIVE IMPOSED ON LIFE, SO EVERYTHING LOGICALLY PROCEEDS TO A TIDY CONCLUSION.

I PREFER TO HAVE LIFE FILTERED THROUGH TELEVISION.

IT'S TOO HARD TO FIGURE OUT! YOU NEVER KNOW WHAT'S GOING ON! YOU DON'T HAVE ANY CONTROL OVER EVENTS!

I DON'T LIKE REAL EXPERIENCE.

AND IF YOU DON'T LIKE WHAT'S HAPPENING, "CLICK." YOU CHANGE THE CHANNEL AND THERE'S SOMETHING DIFFERENT! THAT'S HOW REAL LIFE SHOULD BE.

"CLICK."

WAAA

OH GOOD, A FARCE!

158

LOOK HOW YOUR TAIL FLIPS AROUND!

I WONDER WHICH MUSCLES CONTROL THAT. I CAN SORT OF CLENCH MY BUTT, BUT I DON'T THINK IT COULD WIGGLE A TAIL... HMM, HOW STRANGE!

I'VE NEVER REALLY THOUGHT ABOUT BUTT MUSCLES BEFORE.

SOME THINGS DON'T NEED THE THOUGHT PEOPLE GIVE THEM.

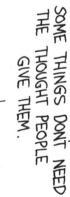

I'M IN A *VERY* BAD MOOD, SO NOBODY'D BETTER MESS WITH ME *TODAY,* BOY!!

HERE, I GOT YOU A NEW COMIC BOOK. WHY DON'T YOU JUST SIT ON THE COUCH AND I'LL MAKE YOU SOME PEANUT BUTTER CRACKERS. ARE YOU COMFY?

UM, I GUESS SO.

MOM KNOWS *EVERYTHING.*

I'M NOT GOING TO DO MY MATH HOMEWORK.

LOOK AT THESE UNSOLVED PROBLEMS. HERE'S A NUMBER IN MORTAL COMBAT WITH ANOTHER. ONE OF THEM IS GOING TO GET SUBTRACTED, BUT WHY? HOW? WHAT WILL BE LEFT OF HIM?

IF I ANSWERED THESE, IT WOULD KILL THE SUSPENSE. IT WOULD RESOLVE THE CONFLICT AND TURN INTRIGUING POSSIBILITIES INTO BORING OL' FACTS.

I NEVER REALLY THOUGHT ABOUT THE LITERARY QUALITIES OF MATH.

I PREFER TO SAVOR THE MYSTERY.

I BET YOU'RE ALL THINKING, "WOW, HOW DID THOSE CLOTHES WALK TO THE FRONT OF THE CLASS ALL BY THEMSELVES?"

AND NOW LOOK! HERE'S A PIECE OF CHALK FLOATING AROUND! PRETTY WEIRD, HUH? YES, FOR SHOW AND TELL TODAY, I, CALVIN, HAVE TURNED MYSELF INVISIBLE!

HA HA! NOW I'LL TAKE OFF THESE CLOTHES AND THE NEXT SOUND YOU HEAR WILL BE MY FEET HEADING FOR THE DOOR! ADIOS, AMIGOS!

LUCKY GUESS, MISS WORMWOOD! WOOOOOOH, THESE PANTS ARE HOVERING OVER THE CLASS! OOOOH!

HELLLPP! MONARCHISTS!

I THEREFORE ASSERT MY PATRIOTIC PREROGATIVE NOT TO KNOW THIS MATERIAL. I'LL BE OUT ON THE PLAYGROUND.

IF IGNORANCE IS BLISS, THIS LESSON WOULD APPEAR TO BE A DELIBERATE ATTEMPT ON YOUR PART TO DEPRIVE ME OF HAPPINESS, THE PURSUIT OF WHICH IS MY UNALIENABLE RIGHT ACCORDING TO THE DECLARATION OF INDEPENDENCE.

MISS WORMWOOD?

YES, CALVIN?

MY BRAIN WISHES MY EGO HAD CALL-WAITING.

OH YEAH?! I'D LIKE TO SEE YOU TRY IT!

I'm gonna pound you in gym class, Twinky.

THERE REALLY OUGHT TO BE A FALL OLYMPICS.

Z
BPBPBBPB
IT'S A HIGH PRICE TO PAY, BUT NUZZLING TIGER TUMMIES IS ONE OF THE GREAT PLEASURES OF LIFE.

171

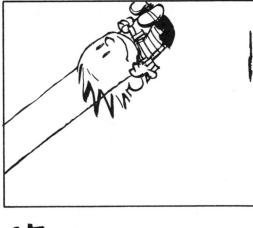

173

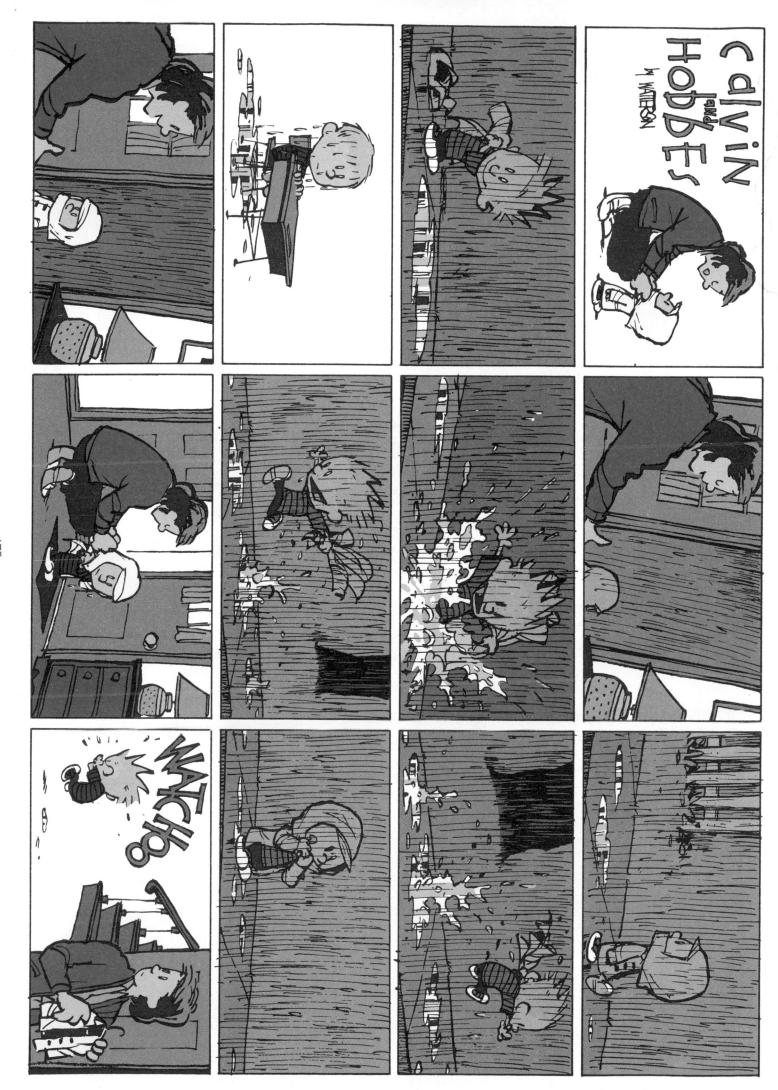